They Saved the Union at Little Round Top

Gettysburg – July 2, 1863

D1202641

by Ken Discorfano

Foreword by John J. Pullen

Property of
Lodi Memorial Library

Thomas Publications
Gettysburg, PA 17325

973.734
DIS

Copyright © 2002 Ken Discorfano

Printed and bound in the United States of America

Published by THOMAS PUBLICATIONS
P.O. Box 3031
Gettysburg, Pa. 17325

All rights reserved. No part of this book may be used or reproduced without written permission of the author and the publisher, except in the case of brief quotations embodied in critical essays and reviews.

ISBN-1-57747-088-5

Cover design by Ryan C. Stouch

Dedicated to

Brig. Gen. Strong Vincent

Commander, Third Brigade, First Division 5th Corps,
U.S. Army of the Potomac — Gettysburg, 1863.

He took the responsibility.

Contents

FOREWORD

Ken Discorfano is not your ordinary author. On one occasion when he was in Maine on a research trip I happened to be with him during his visit to a house in Litchfield once occupied by Andrew Tozier, one of the heroes of Little Round Top. Ken was at the door of the house talking to the current resident while I was sitting in his car some distance away — too far away to hear their conversation. Suddenly it occurred to me that there was a question, central to the research, that he ought to be asking. When he returned to the car I anxiously inquired if he had asked this question. He looked at me a moment, reprovingly I thought, and replied, "Sure I did. I'm a cop — remember?"

Ken is a retired police captain, and I think that what you are about to read will prove that being a police officer is an excellent background for a writer of books about battles.

In both lines of endeavor a frequent question is "Just what really happened here?" And in both cases there are people around with different versions of what took place. Certainly the battle of Little Round Top answers that description. Ever since the last shot was fired on this bloodstained pile of rocks, differing accounts of what happened have been appearing, and they will continue to appear. I doubt that a 100% correct version will ever appear, for the fighting here was so violent and chaotic. The virtue of Ken Discorfano's book, and certain others, is that they keep adding fresh looks at the event and information never before published. Discorfano has gone into some areas that others have not fully explored. For example, as to whether Little Round Top was really an important turning point in the battle, what did top commanders who were actually on the field think? He reproduces some correspondence relating to the promotion of Col. Strong Vincent which was initiated by General Meade on the spot and on the very next day after the fight that goes a long way toward settling that question. Likewise he has investigated and reported on the dramatis personae of the battle — what sort of people were involved, what were their characters before and after the war? — in a way that brings them to life as real people.

How did Ken Discorfano get started on this book? What ignited his interest? This is a question authors are asked, I believe, more often than any other, so we may well apply it here. Again, the background is not what you find in the lives of most authors. After high school and service in the Vietnam War, Discorfano returned to his home town of Lodi, New Jersey, which is about twelve miles from New York, in the heavily populated area surrounding that big city. Shortly afterward he joined the Lodi Police Department. He worked his way up through the ranks and became a captain commanding the patrol division. One day a patrolman in his division who was in the National Guard, knowing that he was a Vietnam veteran, said to him, "Our U. S. Army field manual on leadership talks about a guy in the Battle of Gettysburg named Colonel Joshua Chamberlain who showed great leadership skills."

This remark led Discorfano to an interest in that battle, and a trip to Gettysburg made him an avid student of Chamberlain and his role in the fight on Little Round Top. As the training officer of his police department, he often used the story of Chamberlain at Little Round Top to inspire young officers to think, to take charge in emergency situations and to develop their own leadership skills. Meanwhile his frequent trips to Gettysburg had led him to believe that the full story of the men who fought at Little Round Top had not yet been told. Over the years he did a great deal of research, on the field in company with experienced guides as well as in libraries and archives. He gathered pictures from many sources, had maps done by the noted Gettysburg cartographer John Heiser, and assembled the results in the book you now have in hand. I believe he intended it as a sort of companion book for people visiting the battlefield, but even if you never set foot on this hallowed ground you will find it entertaining and instructive.

John J. Pullen
Brunswick, Maine
January 2002

INTRODUCTION

"And, while all this was going on," explained Gary Kross, "Col. Vincent was trying to shore up the right wing of his brigade on Little Round Top which was faltering; the line of the 44th New York was getting battered while the line of the 16th Michigan just to its right was crumbling! Seeing the trouble developing there, Vincent hurried to urge his men to keep a hot fire on the enemy. It was while so exposed that Vincent was shot through the hip, and went down here," pointing to an area near the base of a boulder near the hilltop, "and was taken back to a safer position of cover. Shortly thereafter, Col. Patrick O'Rorke with his 140th New York regiment, came over the crest, "in the nick of time" and without time to properly load their weapons, fell upon the advancing Confederates and pushed them back. O'Rorke, leading at the front, dropping dead in his tracks with a bullet through his neck!"

Gary Kross is one of the many fine battlefield guides working the field at Gettysburg. If you are in Gettysburg, or plan to go soon, make it a point to contact the Visitor's Center there, and secure the services of one of these. Kross helped light the fire in my mind about Gettysburg and inspired me to learn more about Vincent, O'Rorke, Chamberlain, Warren and others who saved the day—and perhaps the Battle of Gettysburg for the Union.

I was a police officer. I knew the value of talking to people, so I began by reading, then sought out a few of the authors of what I read, and one by one I got to know them. Sometimes they found me at their doorstep. First was John Pullen, famed author of the Civil War classic *The Twentieth Maine: A Volunteer Regiment in the Civil War*, who has been a mainstay helper, encourager, through these years of searching and finding. He read my manuscript and provided invaluable input. We spent time on Little Round Top together. On my way home to New Jersey from one research trip to Bowdoin College in Brunswick, Maine, I stopped in Berlin, Connecticut, and knocked at the door of Willard Wallace, (now late), Professor Emeritus of Wesleyan University in Middletown, and Chamberlain's first biographer. I never attended one of his classes, but perhaps I did better. I was invited into the Wallace home, into their study, and to their table. They shared more than a meal. Will shared his experiences in tracking Chamberlain's compelling story. He became a cheerleader, as historians usually do, for others who want to carry the torch further. Will became fascinated with what I had found and my approach to telling the personal side of the story. Other battlefields too, were discussed.

Archivists like Sylvia Sherman in Augusta, Maine, were cordial and helpful throughout — in state archives, the National Archives, the U. S. Army Military History Institute at Carlisle, and beyond. The West Point Military Academy library staff provided me with a photograph/copy of the original "military pledge" signed by young cadet Patrick O'Rorke upon entering the Military Academy, included herein as a poignant reminder of sacrifices made in the course of doing one's duty. Special materials are affecting; in addition to Chamberlain's letters in Bowdoin College's Special Collections, the staff brought out Chamberlain's Medal of Honor. To hold it was to connect with its story. There are too many to list them all, North and South, from Maine to Texas. They are the same everywhere; helpful, doing their part to keep our nation's history alive. I thank them all.

Thanks to Brian A. Bennett, champion of the 140th New York regiment's history, who helped me find some important photos, particularly of Col. O'Rorke's Clara, the love of his life. Her story is worth illuminating. It shows that war affects us all, many dramatically. Thanks to Jim and Myra Wright, who have been clamoring for recognition for Brig. Gen. Strong Vincent, to whom this book is dedicated. For too long he has been somewhat neglected. They also provided a photo of Vincent's widow, Elizabeth, whose love endured beyond the pain of War. Thanks to Scott Hartwig, Gettysburg historian, and Tom Desjardin, historian and Little Round Top expert, for their feedback and remarks as well. Special thanks to John Heiser, Gettysburg mapmaker, for his detailed maps that depict the field in ways that computer generated maps cannot. And, of course, thanks to Thomas Publications in Gettysburg, for bringing this project to print and to you.

Finally, a special thanks to John and Margaret Pullen. Being shown Chamberlain's pivoting movement by a Chamberlain scholar is an experience I will never forget. For a moment we all slipped away, back to the afternoon of July 2, 1863, to a place in time where the battlefield echoes and the smell of burnt gunpowder filled the air — and for a while we were "there" among the troops. Again, as others before us, we imagined that guttural groan in Chamberlain's voice as it rang out, "Bayonets!" The rest is history. One thing is certain. On this journey I met more than contemporaries, and made more than friends. To one and all, I say thanks for the experience and the memories.

—Ken Discorfano

They Saved the Union at Little Round Top

Meeting the Men

The Prelude to Battle

War is hell! That statement has been made before. But it never rang so true as during the War Between the States, when every muzzle pointed at a brother, father, uncle, or countryman.

Upon looking back to those days of uncertainty and confusion, to find that moment when the scales of victory were tilted, culminating in the Confederate surrender at Appomattox almost two years later, one has but to glance up at that craggy knoll at the southern end of the Union "fish hook" shaped battle line. There on the Union left at Gettysburg, on the afternoon of July 2, 1863, gallant men waged war for its summit, that never-to-be-forgotten battle for Little Round Top!

The actual Battle of Gettysburg, a three-day affair, opened on Wednesday, July 1, 1863, in the early morning when Gen. John Buford's Union cavalry clashed with Confederates under Gen. Henry Heth on McPherson's Ridge west of Gettysburg. Some other Confederate units started coming in northwest of the town and clashed on Oak Hill with Union forces there.

Union General John F. Reynolds, who had a few weeks earlier turned down command of the entire Army of the Potomac, was felled by a sharpshooter's bullet. Shot in the head, he was instantly killed while encouraging his men to hold back the Confederate advance through McPherson's Woods at the opening of the battle. Reynolds' decision to stand and fight at Gettysburg, coupled with outstanding performances by the Iron Brigade, Buford's cavalry and General Abner Doubleday's Division, though they were beaten back and suffered heavy losses on that day, bought valuable time for the newly-appointed commander of the Army of the Potomac, General George G. Meade, to bring up his men and set the stage for the next two days of fighting. And a critical two days they were, for General Robert E. Lee would never again come so close to victory.

As the sun set on July 1, with Union forces beaten back through the town of Gettysburg, they found themselves occupying Cemetery Ridge, a good defensive position, chosen by Gen. O. O. Howard during the retreat. The choice was confirmed by Gen. Winfield S. Hancock, dubbed "Hancock the Superb," by his former chief Gen. George B. McClellan. Hancock was well prepared for his duty. He possessed a masterful military mind.[1]

At about midnight on the night of July 1, Gen. George G. Meade arrived on the field of battle and proceeded to establish himself as a general to be dealt with. He knew Gen. Robert E. Lee from his West Point days. Assessing the situation, Meade decided on a defensive posture of battle, realizing that Lee and his Confederates were on Northern soil and did not have the luxury of waiting. Nor did they have the field advantage that he possessed. Moreover, the good general knew that the price paid by soldiers on the offensive assault was usually a dear one. Meade remembered well the costly lesson learned from attacking the nightmarish "stone wall" at Fredericksburg. This time he would let General Lee's men taste the rain of Union bullets from cover.

At the opening of the second day of the battle, Confederate forces tried the Union left and then the Union right — a tried and true method of winning on the battlefield — turn the enemy flank! But it was not to be. The defensive line set up by Gen. Meade and his command was solid, except in one place. Union Gen. Daniel Sickles, not satisfied with his assigned position of defense, had moved his 10,000 or so men forward approximately one half to three quarters of a mile west toward ground that was a bit higher. This astonished other Union officers and angered Gen. Meade. For in doing so, Sickles created a gap in the line and now Little Round Top was left unprotected, except for a small contingent of signal men posted there. This helped to set the stage for the supreme moment of the battle — the moment of decision for the keepers of the craggy rise where a human "swinging gate" would prove to be the harbinger of things to come for the butternut boys.

Col. Strong Vincent

Strike a figure of a man — a leader of men. Dashing images come to mind — resolute — of military bearing, lean and handsome. Such a man was Colonel Strong Vincent, commander, Third Brigade, First Division, Fifth Corps, Army of the Potomac, on the eve of the Battle of Gettysburg. This battle was particularly important to Vincent, whose home was Erie, Pennsylvania. The Confederates were invading his home soil.

MOLLUS

Col. Strong Vincent

Strong Vincent was born on June 17, 1837, in Waterford, Pa., son of an iron foundry owner. He studied at Erie Academy from 1843-1850. From there he went on to learn the trade of an iron molder at his father's firm, employed in the foundry office as a clerk. He had two brothers and a sister.[2]

In the fall of 1854, he entered Trinity College in Hartford, Connecticut. There he found the affection of Elizabeth H. Carter of Newark, New Jersey, then teaching at Miss Porter's School in nearby Farmington, Connecticut. A long engagement ensued.

After two years at Trinity however, an incident occurred that prompted Vincent to leave the college. A squabble broke out between Vincent and a watchman at Miss Porter's — apparently over the honor of young Miss Carter. A fight resulted, with Vincent standing supreme over the malefactor at its conclusion. He left Trinity shortly afterward, but went to Harvard the next fall. At Harvard he was popular with his classmates and at graduation in 1859, he served as Marshal at Class Day ceremonies.

Upon returning to Erie, Vincent read law at the office of William S. Lane entering the bar in December 1860.[3]

At the outbreak of the Civil War, Vincent promptly enlisted in the Erie regiment organized by Col. John W. McLane. But before he did anything else, he married Elizabeth Carter on April 21, 1861, in Jersey City, New Jersey, and quickly returned to his parents' home on the corner of Peach and Ninth St., in Erie. This would become her new family, as both of her parents had by this time passed away.[4]

As Strong's first ninety-day enlistment came to a close, he reenlisted, this time in the new 83rd Pennsylvania Volunteers formed by

Courtesy Jim and Myra Wright

Elizabeth Carter Vincent

McLane. He was made lieutenant, second in command to the colonel. They mustered in on September 13, 1861.

In June 1862, Vincent contracted Chickahominy Fever (malaria) when the 83rd saw action in the Battle of Gaines's Mill. In the battle Col. McLane was killed, and the regiment took heavy losses. Hearing the news, Vincent ordered his manservant, John Hickey, to bring him a horse. That morning found him at Savage Station, at the head of what was left of the regiment. But he took no part in the Seven Days' Battles. He was too weak.

With McLane's death Vincent was promoted to colonel. He was sent home to Erie to convalesce until mid-October 1862.[5] During this period he suffered from severe urinary tract discomfort as well, probably aggravated from hard riding. Elizabeth and Dr. Brandes, a prominent Erie physician and Vincent family doctor, provided the necessary care to restore his health. Elizabeth's August 6, 1862, letter to Miss Porter reflects this:

> The fever was broken when he reached Jersey City. But then began a slight trouble with the urinary organs. After a few days of fever and only a little delirium he was better... Well, he improved rapidly for a week or so, when suddenly inflammation and hemorrhage of the bladder took place... It will be months before he can go into service....[6]

But Vincent returned to the head of the regiment for the Battle of Fredericksburg in December 1862. Elizabeth visited him in winter quarters at Stoneman's Switch. It is likely that during this time Elizabeth conceived a child, for a daughter was born to them in September 1863. Mrs. Vincent was remembered by Pvt. Oliver W. Norton, Vincent's bugler:

> She was a very handsome young woman, tall, graceful and a superb horsewoman. When his duties permitted, Vincent loved to ride with her through the camps of the Army and the surrounding country. They were followed with looks of admiration wherever they appeared. Their love was ideal.[7]

On or about May 20, 1863, Col. Vincent took command of the Third Brigade, First Division, Fifth Corps, succeeding Col. T. B. W. Stockton who had either resigned or gone on detached service. In the next few weeks, Vincent would be given an opportunity seldom given to an officer of his rank. He would stand with his men on perhaps the most critical part of the battlefield and become the human wall that said, "No!" to Confederate hopes of success at Gettysburg on the second day of the battle. He was just 26 years old.[8]

Gen. Gouverneur K. Warren

Born in the village of Cold Spring, New York, on January 8, 1830, he was the fourth of Sylvanus Warren's brood of twelve children — eight sons and four daughters. He was named for his father's intimate friend Gouverneur Kemble formerly a member of Congress from New York.[9]

Gouverneur Kemble Warren grew up in the legend-haunted highlands of the Hudson, within arrow shot of West Point, just across the Hudson River. After primary school and one year at Kinsley's School near West Point, he received an appointment to the prestigious Military Academy at the age of 16, carrying with him the high expectations of a friend: "We expect you to rank, at graduation, not lower than second," said the kindly Kemble.[10] Young Warren did just that, graduating on July 1, 1850,

National Archives

Gouverneur Kemble Warren

second in his class of 44 polished new 2nd lieutenants, and into the highly specialized engineer corps, generally considered to be the Army's elite corps. In short, his future was looking very bright.

Early assignments sent him to the West, beyond the Mississippi, exploring and mapping the unknown, and even to the Black Hills of Dakota during the Sioux Expedition in 1855, where he got his first glimpse of battle. It was nasty business, but it helped him to develop an eye for terrain, the world of the topographer and mapmaker, which would serve him well at Gettysburg and throughout his military career.[11]

In 1859, however, Warren was assigned to West Point as assistant professor of mathematics. He was relieved to head back home for his father, with whom he had a warm and wonderful relationship, had died. He wanted to be closer to his family, where he could help shoulder family responsibilities. So he took up his post to help train the Army's future leaders — some of whom he would see go into battle with him and some against him, in the not-too-distant future.

Troubles were brewing in the country. Among his students was a young Irish boy, 23-year-old Patrick H. O'Rorke who had started at the Academy two years earlier at the age of 21, a bit older than the rest of the boys in his class. He was a very bright student and demonstrated fine military bearing. But Warren could not have known that he would later order O'Rorke to charge up Little Round Top and into the history of heroes.[12]

In April 1861, after Fort Sumter fell, it seemed that every Army officer was looking for a command. Warren was no different. He was on fire with patriotism. And after weeks of trying to secure a position at the head of a regiment, he took leave of West Point on May 8 and was mustered into the United States service on May 14, 1861, as lieutenant colonel, 5th New York Regiment Vol. Militia.[13]

Warren participated in many battles in the early part of the War and made friends in high places. Shortly after the Peninsula Campaign he was sent with the 5th New York to Baltimore, where he received his promotion to full colonel on August 31, 1861. On September 26, 1862, he was promoted to brigadier general for outstanding performance in the Battle of Gaines's Mill on June 27, 1862 — a promotion pressed for by the commander, George B. McClellan. Warren achieved this milestone at the ripe old age of 32. His skill and determination had paid off. He served at Antietam, Fredericksburg, and Chancellorsville, to name a few of the many battles leading up to the Gettysburg Campaign.

On June 17, 1863, Gouverneur Kemble Warren found the time to take a wife, and married Emily Forbes Chase, a daughter of Algernon Sydney Chase, a dry-goods commission merchant of St. Paul St., Baltimore. They were married in the Chase home drawing room with a reception afterward. But military demands did not allow the couple a long honeymoon, for Warren received orders to immediately return to headquarters. Lee's army was on the move north and arrangements had to be made to give them a welcome they would not soon forget. So the newlyweds kissed goodbye and Warren reported as ordered. Now Warren had more than a flag to fight for. The tender longings of love for his sweet Emily spurred him on even more. He wrote to her almost daily of his whereabouts and activities and looked forward to her letters, the food of lovers apart.[14]

Warren, by Emerson G. Taylor

Emily Forbes Chase Warren

During the next few days, command of the Army of the Potomac would change hands from Gen. Hooker to the steady hand of Gen. George G. Meade. This mattered little to Warren, for he got along well with the higher ups and Meade had great trust in him. Warren was by this time Chief Engineer of the Army, and some even called him Meade's Chief of Staff. Though this was technically the wrong title for him, he acted as such in advising Meade. His guidance in the matter of deciding whether to stay and fight at Gettysburg supported Hancock's decision to do so. This made Meade, who was not on the field of battle at Gettysburg on the first day, more comfortable in the assessment that the Union position was a strong one — so the Union stayed, fought and won. Once again, on the second day of the Battle of Gettysburg, Warren would play a key role in the decision making process. Scanning the battlefield with his well-trained eye he saw the need to protect the Union left at Little Round Top, for the moment vacant of troops, yet the key to the whole position.

Col. Joshua L. Chamberlain

"Do it! That's how!" said the firm father of young Joshua Lawrence Chamberlain, when their hay wagon was stuck in the bed of a stream, wedged between two tree stumps and the puzzled nineteen year old boy asked, "How am I going to do it?" "The youth seized the hub, lifted the wheel clear of the stump and threw it over with such force that the cart-tongue knocked against the nose of the "off ox" and the whole team was off in a jiffy." And that was the maxim he learned to live by. It served him well.[15]

Born in Brewer, Maine, on September 8, 1828, Joshua Lawrence Chamberlain was the son of a farmer. His father once commanded the militia regiment sent eastward by Governor John Fairchild at the time of Maine's famous "Aroostook War" with New Brunswick. Lawrence, as he was affectionately called by his parents, had three brothers and a sister.[16]

Young Lawrence acquired a fine education at Bowdoin College in Brunswick, Maine, and then completed studies in theology at the Bangor Theological Seminary in the fall of 1852. That he mastered several languages, including French, German, Latin, Hebrew, Syriac and Greek, in the course of his studies is evidence of his intellectual prowess and determination. Upon completion of his studies he took a position instructing Logic and Natural Theology at Bowdoin. He then married Fanny Adams, a fellow parishioner at the First Parish Church in Brunswick, near Bowdoin College, on December 7, 1855. Four children were born to them, but only two survived; Grace Dupee, whom Chamberlain affectionately called Daisy, and Harold Wyllys.[17]

At Bowdoin, the Chamberlains enjoyed a comfortable life, living in a lovely home on Potter St. near the campus, close to their church and friends, until the War began.

Although the college administration told him that he was far more valuable to his country as a professor, Chamberlain could not help being drawn to what he thought was the higher duty to country — being a soldier. He made an appointment to see Governor Washburn and offered his services. Commissioned a Lieutenant Colonel of the new 20th Maine Regiment, he mustered into service in August 1862. Quickly, Chamberlain started reading books on battle tactics and military matters. He stayed close to the regiment's colonel, Adelbert Ames, a West Point graduate and winner of the Medal of Honor for

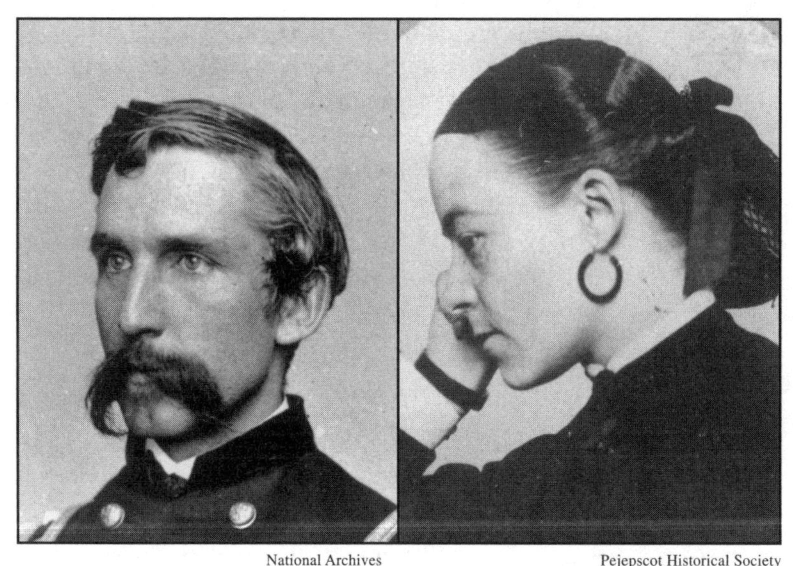

National Archives

Joshua L. Chamberlain

Pejepscot Historical Society

Frances "Fanny" Adams Chamberlain

heroism at the First Battle of Bull Run. Chamberlain, always the good student, learned fast under the tutelage of his able colonel and together they molded the men into a well disciplined fighting force.[18]

At the Battle of Antietam on September 17, 1862, the 5th Corps was left in reserve and did not see action, but at Fredericksburg they became combat veterans. In a December chill, Union troops were fodder for the Confederate artillery, subjected to a relentless blaze of fire and smoke from the gray coats behind the unforgettable Stone Wall. Chamberlain later remembered:

> We had to pick our way over a field strewn with incongruous ruin; men torn and broken and cut to pieces in every indescribable way, cannon dismounted, gun carriages smashed or overturned, ammunition chests flung wildly about, horses dead and half-dead, still held in harness, accouterments of every sort scattered as by whirlwinds. It was not good for the nerves, that ghastly march, in the lowering night![19]

In mid-April 1863, an epidemic of smallpox hit the 20th Maine so hard that they were quarantined and left to guard telegraph lines instead of participate in the Battle of Chancellorsville. Colonel Ames somehow got himself attached to 5th Corps Commander Gen. Meade's staff at that time and won promotion to brigadier general for his effort in the battle. Joshua L. Chamberlain was then promoted to full colonel to fill the vacancy, taking command of the regiment effective June 23, 1863, as Brig. Gen. Ames departed to command elsewhere.[20]

Chamberlain, affected by sunstroke earlier that month, was recovered and at the lead of the regiment in the closing days of June 1863, when the Army of the Potomac anticipated Lee's steps onto Northern soil where they would meet at the small crossroads town of Gettysburg. He was 34 years old.[21]

Col. Patrick H. O'Rorke

Patrick Henry O'Rorke was born on March 28, 1836, in County Cavern, Ireland. When he was about one year old his parents, Patrick Sr. and Mary Merger O'Rorke moved the family to Montreal. After a short stay there, they moved to Oswego, New York, briefly and finally took up permanent residence on Emmett St., in Rochester, New York's "Dublin" section of town. They were among the many Irish immigrants then populating the town.[22]

He received his education at "Old Number Nine," the nearby public school. His later school records are missing, but in 1855 Patrick competed in an open competition for two possible scholarships at the University of Rochester. He placed first but declined the scholarship at the objection of his mother, who as a devout Catholic was disturbed by the denominational control of the University. Probably, Patrick gave in to his mother's wishes out of respect. His father had been killed in a work-related accident when Patrick was only fourteen, and his mother's wishes probably carried the weight of his absent father as well. Instead, Patrick took an apprenticeship at the Hibbard Marble Works in Rochester, to learn the trade of a stone cutter. He took quickly to the mastery of the trade.[23]

Regarding his appointment to the Military Academy — it was not just luck but fate at work in the matter. It seems that the Hon. John Williams, Member of Congress for Monroe and Orleans Counties, was having difficulty in finding boys who could pass muster at West Point; his previous appointees had apparently failed to make the grade. Frustrated and somewhat embarrassed, he turned to Rochester School Commissioner Samuel G. Andrews to recommend a youth who could succeed. O'Rorke's name came to the fore and an appointment was offered and accepted. On June 11, 1857, Patrick H. O'Rorke reported to the Military Academy to begin his studies with $60.00 in his pocket. Coincidentally, another new cadet arriving a week earlier had reported having the same amount on hand. This was the young 17 year old George A. Custer. But the pocket cash varied.[24]

U.S. Military Institute

Young Patrick Henry O'Rorke

The document copy of Patrick H. O'Rorke's U.S. Military Academy Pledge, poignantly signed with the consent of his mother, is included here as a stark reminder of a commitment so dutifully kept.

Patrick O'Rorke was not born with a silver spoon in his mouth. And though many people of means and status exerted influence to garner appointments for favorite sons and friends, O'Rorke's class was a good mix of society from all quarters. He was Irish and the Irish had a reputation for being a bit wild. Patrick, however, displayed none of the stereotypical traits and propelled himself to the top of his class — first among his peers.

Upon graduation from the West Point Military Academy, newly commissioned 2nd Lt. O'Rorke found himself drilling troops in the national capital — Washington. At the First Battle of Bull Run, on July 21, 1861, his horse was shot from under him. He narrowly missed being wounded as a bullet passed through his coat but missed his body. On March 15, 1862, he was promoted to Brevet Captain for merit.[25]

On July 9, 1862, Patrick married Clara Wadsworth Bishop at St. Bridget's Church in Rochester while home on leave. They had been childhood sweethearts, schoolmates, and fellow parishioners at St. Bridget's, where she was the organist and sang in the choir. Theirs was a wonderful relationship, long founded on love and deeply rooted in faith. Their love was ideal.[26]

United States Military Academy
West Point N.Y. July 1st 1857.

I Patrick H O'Rorke of the State of New York aged Twenty years, Eleven months, having been selected for an appointment as Cadet in the Military Academy of the United States, do hereby engage, with the consent of my Mother, in the event of my receiving such appointment, that I will serve in the Army of the United States for eight years, unless sooner discharged by competent authority. And I Patrick H. O'Rorke do solemnly swear, that I will bear true faith and allegiance to the United States of America, and that I will serve them Honestly and Faithfully against all their enemies or opposers whatsoever, and that I will observe and obey the orders of the President of the United States, and the orders of the Officers appointed over me, according to the Rules and Articles of War. Patrick H. O'Rorke

Sworn and subscribed to, at West Point, New York, this Sixth day of February Eighteen hundred and Fifty Eight before me Chas. Drake

Clerk of Orange County

U.S. Military History Institute (West Point).

Cadet Patrick H. O'Rorke's West Point Military Academy Pledge — a poignant reminder of a promise made…a promise kept.

On September 8, 1862, Patrick was commissioned Col. Patrick H. O'Rorke and detached to the 140th New York Regiment of Volunteers. Now he sported fashionable side burns, intending, it was said, to make himself look a little older. He was 26 years old.[27]

Patrick's firm discipline with the men of the 140th New York enabled him to develop them into a fine fighting force. Present at Fredericksburg on December 11-15, 1862, they were held in reserve and saw no action. They did, however, see action at the Battle of

Courtesy Michael Albanese Collection

Clara Wadsworth Bishop O'Rorke

Chancellorsville on May 1-3, 1863. O'Rorke's actions were recognized when he received a promotion to lieutenant colonel in his regular branch (the Engineers).

Colonel O'Rorke was not known to make long and winded speeches to his men. When he delivered the pre-Battle of Gettysburg speech to his comrades, he called on every man to do his duty — lest he be shot! An echo of Gen. Meade's compelling order, it recognized the import of the situation. And it was bone chilling in its effect. The men could do nothing but respect and admire their leader — and they proved it by following him into the very jaws of death on that fateful afternoon on Little Round Top.[28]

Sgt. Andrew J. Tozier

Andrew J. Tozier was born on February 11, 1838, in Monmouth, Maine, near Litchfield. Nothing much is known of his early childhood years except that as a young boy he ran away from home to become a sailor.

In 1861, Andrew returned home to his family, then living in Plymouth. When the cry of "War!" was sounded Andrew, like thousands of others, responded. On July 15, 1861, Andrew mustered into the ranks of the 2nd Maine regiment as a private. He was promoted to the rank of corporal sometime in January or February of 1862.[29]

During the Battle of Gaines's Mill on June 27, 1862, Andrew received a painful wound in his left ankle, (the bullet entering but not exiting), a broken rib and loss of the middle finger of his left hand. He was captured and spent time in two Confederate prisons in Richmond before being exchanged and finding his way back into the Union ranks. He must have been thinking he had a "personal" score to settle. On January 1, 1863, records reflect his promotion to the rank of first sergeant.[30]

On May 20, 1863, Sgt. Tozier was transferred to Company I, 20th Maine Infantry, along with several other members of the 2nd Maine. It seems that there was some controversy over the actual enlistment agreement signed by the men. Through an error of explanation or some other misunderstanding, these men had signed enlistment papers for three years' duty, thinking that their enlistment was for two years. As some of the other Maine boys began packing up to head home, they naturally expected to follow. However, upon review of the documents, it was determined that they had one more year of service to give. They were not happy, and they refused duty.

Tozier found himself among this unhappy group of transferees sent to Col. Joshua L. Chamberlain of the 20th Maine Regiment. Chamberlain had orders to shoot any of the soldiers who refused to fight. But he did not want to shoot any Union men, especially boys from his own home state. Understanding their grievance, he told them that he would look into the matter, but in the meantime he expected every man to do his duty.

Chamberlain had a way with men. It showed at Gettysburg, a little over a month later, when these men from the Pine Tree State provided the necessary punch needed to help win the day.[31]

On June 29, the color sergeant of the regiment, Sgt. Charles Proctor, got drunk, was insubordinate to his superiors and was arrested. Tozier, next ranking sergeant, was given command of the colors. And for his work on that hot and sticky July 2 afternoon at Little Round Top, Andrew J. Tozier would receive the nation's highest salute — the Medal of Honor.[32]

THE BATTLE

The Federal Left

The morning of July 1 found Col. Strong Vincent and his brigade of the Fifth Corps marching from Maryland onto Pennsylvania soil, in pursuit of Lee who appeared to be heading toward Baltimore:

> Col. Vincent sent back word to the regiment that we were now on the soil of old Pennsylvania — to hang out the banner on the outward wall, and let our march be accompanied by the sound of the ear-piercing fife and spirit-stirring drum.[33]

They marched to Yankee Doodle, which ran through the line brigade by brigade. Soon the Pennsylvania hills were alive with the sound. Late that afternoon as they reached Hanover they received news of the First Corps clash to the north, of General John F. Reynolds being killed at the front with his men, and of superior forces pushing back Union troops. Everyone was now converging on a small town in south central Pennsylvania hitherto unknown, but soon never-to-be-forgotten — Gettysburg![34]

Already signs of battle were visible. General Kilpatrick's cavalry had a few hours before encountered Gen. J. E. B. Stuart's Confederate cavalry and driven them back near Hanover. "Dead horses — and corpses of cavalrymen staring fixedly at the sky as though they had seen a wonder that words could not tell."[35] They were allowed a brief few hours to rest and then put on the march again. Off in the distance the roll of cannon thunder could be heard.

The citizens came out to cheer them on, some in patriotism and some out of fear. They were not used to seeing the war except on the front pages of their newspapers. Now, it had come to their own neighborhood. A group of girls by the wayside began singing:

> ...The Star Spangled Banner, and Col. Vincent pulled out of the column to watch the brigade go by, removed his hat as the colors passed, observed the moonlight shining on the flags, the marching troops, the white dresses of the girls, and, turning to an aide, said that a man could do worse than die fighting under the colors here in Pennsylvania.

Vincent was a young man with a wife six months pregnant back home in Erie. The air and the mood were heavy.[36]

Colonel Joshua L. Chamberlain of the 20th Maine was cognizant of their mood. There seemed to be a magical air about this Army of the Potomac, as rumors flitted up and down the line:

> At the turn of the road a staff officer, with an air of authority, told each colonel as he came up, that McClellan was in command again, and riding ahead of us on the road. Then wild cheers rolled from the crowding column in the brooding sky, and the earth shook under the quickened tread. Now from a dark angle of the roadside came a whisper, whether from earthly or unearthly voice one cannot feel quite sure, that the august form of Washington had been seen that afternoon at sunset riding over the Gettysburg hills.

The enthusiasm and excitement of the men soared. Vincent himself caught the moment. Raising his hand and waving he exclaimed, "Now boys, we will give 'em hell tomorrow." Of course, the reports of McClellan being put back in charge and of Washington being seen riding on the battlefield were not true. And it never was determined from where they had originated, but such was the level of excitement among the ranks.[37]

In line too, was Col. Patrick H. O'Rorke, in command of the 140th New York Regiment. The 140th was in the 2nd Division, 3rd Brigade of the Fifth Corps, under the command of Gen. Stephen H. Weed, another West Pointer. Their new corps commander, Maj. Gen. George Sykes had filled the position vacated by Maj. Gen. George G. Meade a few days earlier when the latter was given command of the entire Army of the Potomac by a hopeful president. The Corps halted about two miles from Gettysburg near midnight and the soldiers were allowed to fall out and sleep for a few hours. Captain Leeper laid his poncho next to O'Rorke's but neither was able to sleep much. The two men "talked over the probable events of the day, he (O'Rorke) seeming to have foreboding anticipations."[38] At 3:30 a.m. reveille was sounded and within an hour they were allowed to rest. After several changes in their position they finally crossed Rock Creek on the Baltimore Pike about 8:00 a.m. and went into mass formation near Powers Hill, where they were well located to reinforce quickly any part of the main line.[39]

Shortly after taking command a few days earlier, Meade issued his urgent order. Colonel O'Rorke handed the circular to his adjutant, Lt. Porter Farley, to be read to the men. The order read:

> The Commanding General requests that previous to the engagement soon expected with the enemy corps and all other commanding officers will address their troops, explaining to them briefly the immense issues involved in the struggle. The enemy are on our soil. The whole country now looks anxiously to this Army to deliver it from the presence of the foe. Our failure to do so will leave us no such welcome as the swelling of millions of hearts with pride and joy at our success would give to every soldier in the Army. Homes, firesides, and domestic altars are involved. The Army has fought well before. It is believed that it will fight more desperately and bravely than ever if it is addressed in fitting terms.
>
> Corps and other commanders are authorized to order the instant death of any soldier who fails in his duty at this hour. By Command of Major General Meade.[40]

Colonel Patrick O'Rorke was not in the habit of making speeches, but this time he sensed the urgency and backed up the order. And "sitting on his little brown horse in front of the regimental colors, dressed as we all so well remember him in his soft, felt hat, long white leather gloves and military cape," O'Rorke addressed his men. His talk was short and to the point, recalled one member of his audience; "he said that we were about to meet the enemy; he wanted every man to do his duty; any man that started to run, be he private or officer, let him die the death of a coward — shoot him on the spot!"[41]

"Those were the words of a man who meant to do his duty, and was resolved that everyone under his command should do the same. The episode was dramatic to the highest degree," remembered Lt. Porter Farley of the 140th New York. A low murmur moved among the crowd. Let no man think he could shirk his duty now — at another man's expense. At times like these unit solidarity began to swell. And so it was settled as the 140th New York and the rest of the Fifth Corps, braced for battle.[42]

The Union battle line on the second day at Gettysburg, formed the pattern of an upside down "fish hook," with Culp's Hill and Cemetery Hill at the north — or hook end — and Big Round Top and Little Round Top at the south — or shank end. On this second day of battle, Lee would try both ends. By turning either or both of these flanks, Lee would have succeeded. The north end, or right of the Union line was stronger than the left, due to the actions of Maj. Gen. Daniel Sickles, Third Corps commander, who acting without orders, moved his Corps forward (facing west) approximately one half to

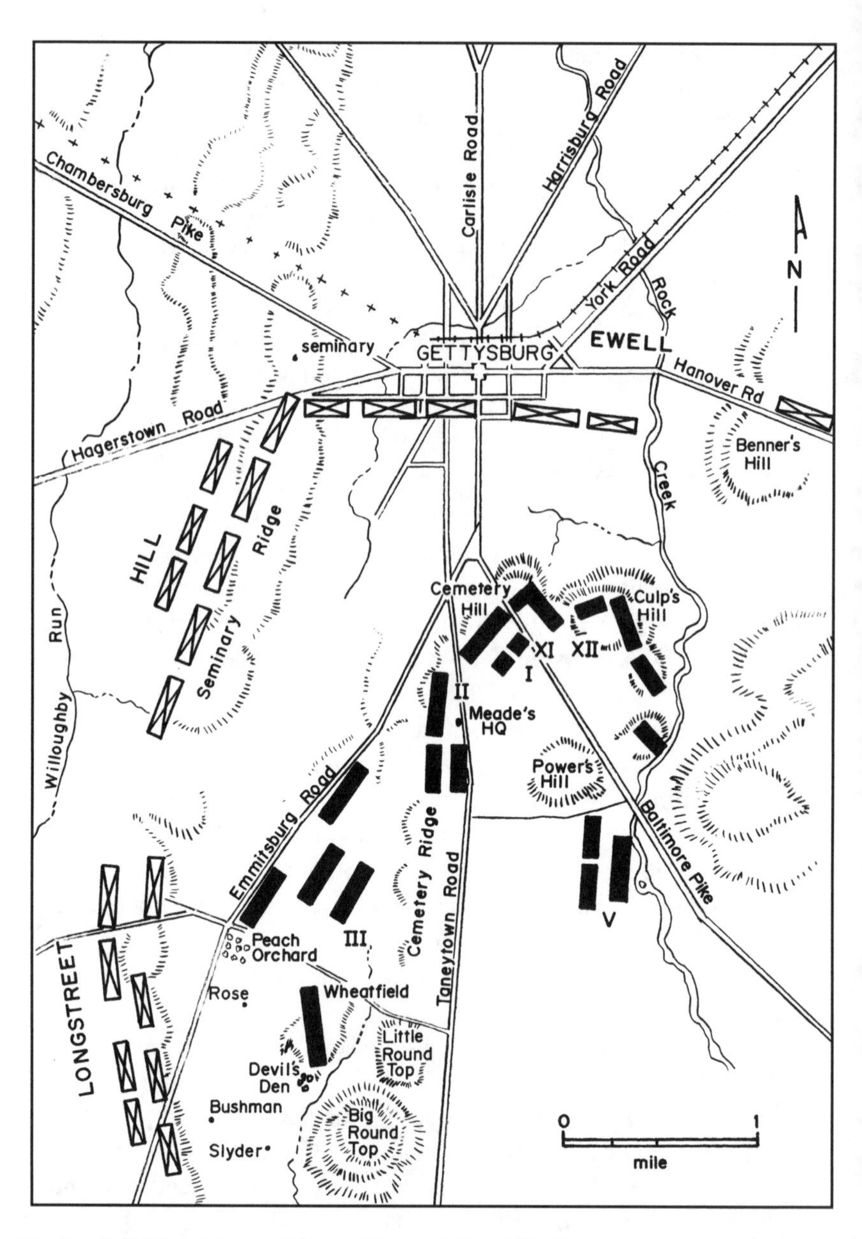

The Battlefield, 3:30 p.m. The positions of the Fifth Corps, near Powers Hill, and Longstreet's near the Emmitsburg Road, just prior to the sequence of battle action that leads to the Battle of Little Round Top. (Note: Times are in Eastern Standard Time. Daylight savings time was not in use during the Civil War. Sunset at Little Round Top would be approximately 7:29 p.m. on July 2nd, 1863).

three quarters of a mile, and in doing so exposed Little Round Top and Big Round Top — left uncovered as a result. This battle tactic itself has been the focus of much historical bantering, for it successfully upset Lee's plan of attack, while it left open another door of opportunity. That the Union succeeded at Gettysburg allowed laurels to later fall on Sickles. Had they lost, Sickles would surely have earned the horns of the goat for his reckless actions that day. But there on the Union left was the golden chance for Lee. He was slow to grasp it — and missed it by about ten minutes.

During that momentous afternoon, Gen. Meade, probably while riding along the line of Cemetery Ridge with his staff which included trusted Brig. Gen. Gouveneur K. Warren, Chief of Engineers, surveyed the situation and said, "Warren! I hear a little peppering going on in the direction of the hill off yonder. I wish that you would ride over and if anything serious is going on…attend to it."[43]

So much was Warren trusted by Meade that upon taking command of the Army, Meade offered him a position as Chief of Staff. Warren declined in consideration of Gen. Dan Butterfield whom he knew and respected — though it would have meant another "star" on his shoulders. Warren was ambitious but thought he was more valuable to Meade and the Army in his present position of Chief Engineer.[44] Also, he was satisfied — a young Brigadier and a newlywed of just two weeks, his career was on a fast track. Warren lit out for Little Round Top with his aides, Lt. Ranald S. Mackenzie, Lt. Chauncey B. Reese, and Lt. Washington A. Roebling (the latter made famous for his participation in the building of the Brooklyn Bridge in New York City after the Civil War — an engineering marvel of the time).[45]

About this time the Confederate guns opened on Sickles' Third Corps at the Peach Orchard and Devil's Den, as Gen. Meade was discussing Sickles' deployment variations with him. With no time to reform the line to conform with Meade's original battle plan, they would have to stay and fight it out. Meade promised support from both the Second and Fifth Corps and Gen. Hunt's artillery. The Union left was on fire.

Upon reaching the summit of Little Round Top, which rose about 170 ft. above the battlefield, Warren was shocked to see just a small contingent of signal men there. His keen eye for topography told him that it was "the key to the whole position." Looking south and

Photo by Author

Gen. Gouverneur K. Warren statue on Little Round Top today. As Chief of Engineers, Warren knew the importance of "high ground." Holding Little Round Top would be the key to the battle.

west he could see a long line of woods east of the Emmitsburg Road which could provide good cover for any enemy force approaching from that direction. This troubled him. Warren then directed a captain of an artillery battery, (probably Smith's Battery), just in front of Little Round Top to fire a shot into those woods. The lone shot whistled through the air and crashed into the woods, causing Confederate troops moving among the trees to react. The sunlight glinted off their gun barrels giving their position away. A movement to turn the Union left was under way.[46]

Warren immediately sent Lt. Mackenzie for a brigade of Sickles' Third Corps, for they were close at hand.[47] Sickles refused this request stating his men were heavily engaged and no troops could be spared. Mackenzie then found Gen. Sykes, Fifth Corps Commander, who assented, promising to send a brigade. A staff officer was dispatched to locate Gen. Barnes with the order.[48] General Sykes had been told by Meade after a 3:00 a.m. meeting at Meade's headquarters at the Leister House to put his entire Corps in on the Union left and to hold that ground "at all hazards."[49] The order was given and the Fifth Corps started to move up as Gen. Sykes rode ahead to survey the ground — probably going to the area of Devil's Den for he saw a gap there.[50] Minutes later, Sykes sent Capt. William Jay off to bring up Barnes' Division. Barnes' troops, with Col. Strong Vincent's Brigade in the lead, approached the battlefield by way of the Granite Schoolhouse Lane and crossed the Taneytown Road; Vincent's Brigade had halted to await orders near the George Weikert house on Cemetery Ridge.[51]

Coming from the front, one of Sykes' aides, possibly Capt. John Williams, was spotted by Vincent. He spurred his horse in the rider's direction to meet him when a charged conversation ensued. "Captain, what are your orders?" The captain replied, "Where is Gen. Barnes?" The captain answered, "Gen. Sykes told me to direct Gen. Barnes to send one of his brigades to occupy that hill yonder," pointing to Little Round Top. Vincent said, "I will take the responsibility of taking my brigade there."[52]

Colonel Vincent returned to the brigade and ordered Col. James C. Rice, the next senior colonel, to lead the brigade to the hill as fast as possible, then rode on ahead to reconnoiter the position so that dispositions could be made. Vincent, with his color bearer, Pvt. Oliver W. Norton, dutifully at his side, brigade flag in hand, (a triangular white flag with a dark blue border and red Maltese cross in the center), galloped to the foot of the hill. Thinking it impossible to ride up to the top in that direction, due to the steepness of the slope there, they turned left and skirted the ridge disappearing into the woods on the eastern side of Little Round Top, following the base of the hill around to the south end. There Vincent began to survey the ground to take advantage as he could of natural barriers, to set up his defense of the hill. It was time for critical thinking, something for which the boys at Harvard Yard had come to be known and respected. And on this day, Strong Vincent would demonstrate his intellectual and military skills.[53]

The brigade followed crossing Plum Run on a crude wooden bridge and turned left onto a farm road that led to the base of the hill. With Col. James C. Rice in the lead, the men of the brigade scurried to go around the northwest base of Little Round Top. Probably by this time Col. Vincent and his flag were out of their view, but Col. Rice knew his objec-

MOLLUS

James C. Rice, 44th New York.

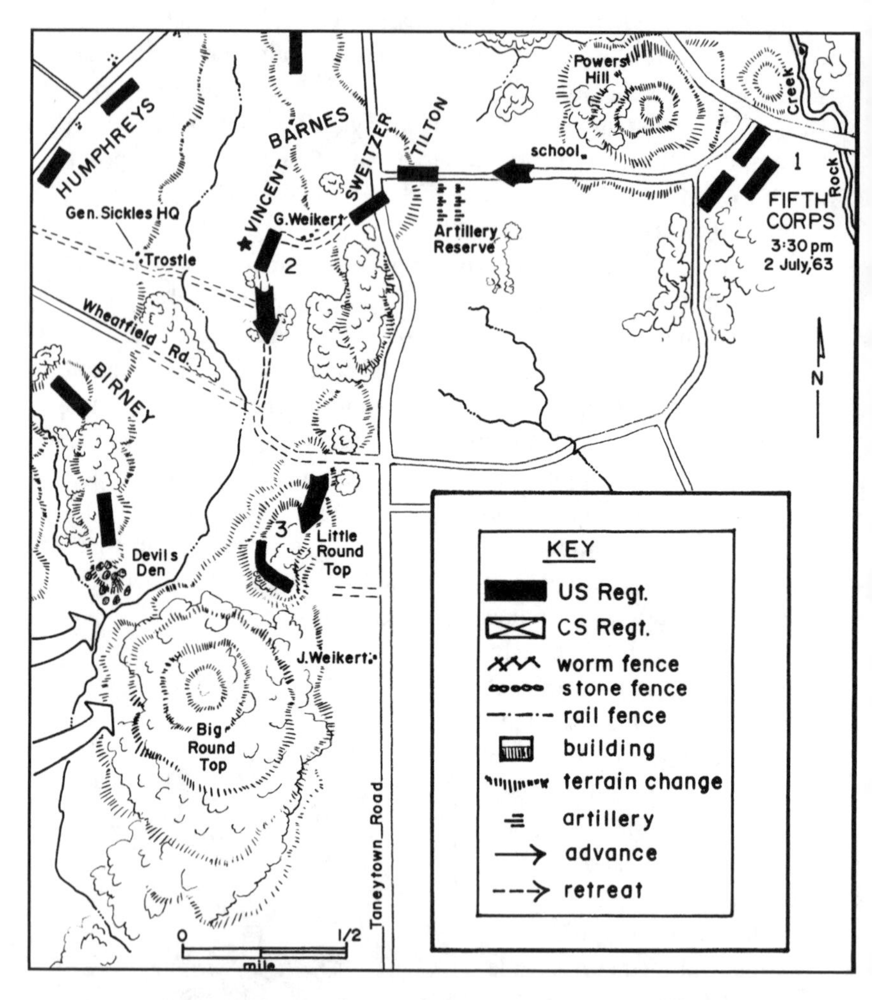

"Captain! What are your orders?" Approx. 4:30 p.m.

1. Fifth Corps, massed at Powers Hill in reserve. 2. At 4:00 p.m., Vincent's Brigade and others are ordered to the front. Moving at the double quick on the Granite School House Lane, then crossing the Taneytown Road, they made their way past the G. Weikert farm into an open field and stopped to wait for orders, placing them on the line. Here, Col. Vincent saw one of Gen. Sykes' aides riding toward him. Vincent utters his famous, "Captain! What are your orders?" 3. Col. Vincent takes the initiative and orders his brigade to Little Round Top, to secure the Union Left.

tive. It was at this point that he directed his troops up the eastern slope at an angle to the southwest, heading for the crest. Following a crude logging trail on the eastern side of the hill, they made their way under cover of the summit. Shells whistled overhead. "Here as we could," said Col. Chamberlain "we took the double quick." Chamberlain did not like what he saw of the hill, an eminence strewn with great boulders, intersected with jagged ledges, bald on top and only a few gnarled trees straggling along the sides.[54] But seeing the troop movements heading for Little Round Top alerted the Confederates that even unseen targets groping along the eastern shoulder of the hill might be hit. And as the Union troops strained to scale the hill enemy gunners got their range and shells came crashing down upon them. Shells burst overhead in the trees causing branches to break, limbs to fall, sending showers of debris all along the line. Suddenly, a solid shot swept close to the heads of Col. Chamberlain and his two brothers, Thomas, the regimental adjutant and a lieutenant, and John, who was serving with the Sanitary Commission. "Boys," Chamberlain said, "I don't like this. Another shot might make it hard for mother. Tom, go to the rear of the regiment and see that it is well closed up! John, pass up ahead and look out for a place for our wounded." Charging up the slope, they felt the concussion of the shells as they exploded and tasted the burnt gunpowder mixed with earthen spray.[55]

Colonel Vincent, having rapidly gone to the right, came out on the little plateau in the rear of the position held later by the 16th Michigan. A Confederate battery which had been firing at the few signal men waving their flags to their right, (Warren's position on Little Round Top), saw Norton's Brigade flag and started firing at them. The colonel got excited when two shells crashed near him and his flag bearer. Quickly dismounting "Old Jim," Vincent yelled, "Down with that flag, Norton! Damn it, go behind the rocks with it!" Norton complied, taking the reins of the colonel's horse as Vincent went down the slope among the rocks to select a position for the brigade — an ingenious battlefield tactic for defense. In this way, if any attacking Confederate force proved too much for the Union men, the troops could fall back to regroup without being driven from the summit. The order of ascent up the hill has been variously reported and a good argument can be made for a few of these, yet not one of them is without its problems. Nevertheless, Col. Rice got the brigade up in good order.[56]

(Left)
Lt. Thomas D. Chamberlain, 20th Maine. Maine State Archives

(Right) Oliver W. Norton in lieutenant's uniform, Dec. 1863. He was a private and Vincent's bugler at Gettysburg.

Courtesy James Wright

(Left) John C. Chamberlain, member of the Christian Commission. These volunteers cared for the spiritual needs of the soldiers and also assisted with the wounded on the battlefield. Pejepscot Historical Society

Upon meeting Col. Vincent on the south side of the hill, Col. Rice was directed to position his 44th New York regiment on the brigade right, an exposed area near the crest amidst large rocks and boulders facing southwest towards Devil's Den. Vincent pointed out a large rock formation where he wished Rice to secure the right of his line. Colonel Rice and his men moved out. And then the rest of the brigade uncurled to the left, the line following the contour of the hill, sloping diagonally downward from the crest; the 83rd Pennsylvania, 20th Maine and finally the 16th Michigan moving into the swale at the eastern base of Little Round Top. Those regiments at the crest moved about one quarter the way down the hill in a military deployment. Quickly, men began throwing up breastworks in preparation for battle.

As this was being accomplished and commanders started ordering their skirmish lines forward, Col. Strong Vincent must have noticed a gap between the 44th New York and the 83rd Pennsylvania, the latter regiment having formed in a rather half circle or bowed line a bit further down the hill, not tying up properly with either the 44th New York on their right nor the 20th Maine on the left. Also, from Vincent's position, he probably saw Confederate troop movements on the brigade right signaling that an attack from that quarter was imminent.

Seeing that his line was spread too wide, Col. Vincent sought to shore it up by moving the 16th Michigan from the far left, ordering them to double quick to fill the gap between the 44th New York and the 83rd Pennsylvania.

Lt. Col. Norval E. Welch of the 16th Michigan had just ordered two of his largest companies, Co. A and Brady's Sharpshooter Co., to go forward as skirmishers, but it has been a matter of debate since, whether those troops went out on the left, or the right, or even if they went out at all. But Welch dutifully obeyed Vincent's order and pulled his men out of the swale at the southeastern base of Little Round Top and headed for the higher ground.[57]

When Welch and his men appeared on the right, Col. Rice appealed to Vincent. "In every battle in which we have engaged, the Eighty-Third and the Forty Fourth have fought side by side. I wish it might be so to-day." Vincent understood, for the two regiments had come to be known as the "Butterfield Twins," after their former commander, Gen. Daniel Butterfield, now Meade's Chief of Staff. "All

MOLLUS

Lt. Col. Norval E. Welch

right, let the Sixteenth pass you," said Vincent. And Col. Rice shifted his men toward the left, filling the gap and put out Capt. Larrabee and his Company B skirmishers to the front. And on they came. The final placement set the 16th Michigan, under Lt. Norval E. Welch with approximately 150 to 200 men on the right flank of Little Round Top. On the left was Col. James C. Rice's 44th New York with about 321 men, then the 83rd Pennsylvania with Capt. O. S. Woodward in command of roughly 274 muskets and on the extreme left, further down the spur — near the saddle between the Round Tops — the 20th Maine, under command of Col. Joshua L. Chamberlain with their 358 guns. Chamberlain had ordered his regiment in "on the right by file into line," thus enabling each man to be ready to fire upon placement on the line. He quickly summoned Capt. Walter G. Morrill to take his Company B men out on the left as skirmishers and to guard against any possible flank attack from that quarter. Morrill took his 50 men and disappeared into the woods to the left of his regiment's position with the initial intention of tying up with the two companies of skirmishers that had gone out from the 16th Michigan. Instead, they found themselves alone — but only for a while.[58]

Chamberlain looked about, studying the terrain. Big Round Top loomed in front and nothing, nothing in the way of support was on his left. Quickly he ordered the right of his line to anchor to the left of the 83rd Pennsylvania. This was done but imperfectly. Then, Vincent came upon him and said, "I place you here! This is the left of the Union line. You understand. You are to hold this ground at all costs!" Chamberlain understood the gravity of the situation and braced himself for the fight of his life.[59]

The line was set–the die cast. There was last minute fidgeting on the line as the Union soldiers grappled with equipment and quickly set up breastworks or covered themselves otherwise behind rocks, boulders, or trees, while looking nervously to front, to catch the first glimpse of the approaching foe. It was about 4:45 p.m. [60]

Hood's Division, 4:00 p.m.

At about 4:00 p.m., Confederate Gen. John B. Hood's Division on the Confederate right, moved to make a frontal attack on the Union left. These were Lee's orders despite requests and recommendations from some of his finest generals including Longstreet, Hood, and even Brig. Gen. Evander M. Law, to try to flank the Union by attacking around the Round Tops, in the hope of turning the Union left, forcing the Union to change fronts, then giving the Confederates the field advantage. Both Hood and Law had learned through field intelligence that there were no troops on the Round Tops and that Federal supply wagons were parked on the east side of those hills — and were lightly guarded.[61]

General Law was not only handsome but intelligent as well. Born in South Carolina in 1836, he was a graduate of the prestigious Citadel. The former principal of a military school in Tuskegee, Alabama, he had a watchful eye for details and had garnered critical field intelligence from captured prisoners and his own scouts, that should have caused Lee to modify his plan. But Lee had made up his mind.[62]

Mollus

Brig. Gen. Evander M. Law

Brigadier Gen. Jerome B. Robertson's Texas Brigade of 1,100 men was lined up with the 3rd Arkansas regiment on the brigade left and the 1st, 4th, and 5th Texas regiments to the right. Brig. Gen. Evander M. Law's Brigade, 1,500 strong, continued the alignment on the right of Robertson's men with the 4th, 47th, 15th, 44th ,and 48th Alabama regiments respectively. The men of Law's Brigade had marched 28 miles that morning in eleven hours to reach the battlefield, later said by Oates to be, "the best marching in either army, to reach the field of Gettysburg." His men were tired and thirsty, but they still had the fighting spirit to go on. Lee's right hand moved into action from a place on Seminary Ridge about 500 yards south of the Emmitsburg Road. And at the head of his 15th Alabama was Col. William C. Oates. While other Confederate leaders would figure dimly in the results at Little Round Top, Col. Oates would be prominent in the ill-fated fortunes of the day on the extreme Confederate right.[63]

Born on November 30, 1833, Col. William C. Oates was 29 years old at Gettysburg. He had a tough life but scratched his way through from a boy who ran away from an abusive father, having scrapes with the law, to working as a painter for $2.50 a day. Despite a sparse education, he managed to prepare himself to pass the bar exam and opened his own law office in Abbeville, Alabama, on his 25th birthday. He was 6'2" in height and well built — he was a scrapper.[64]

Alabama Dept. of Archives and History

Col. William C. Oates, 15th Alabama.

Just before Oates' regiment "stepped off" in the attack, he went to visit with his brother, Lt. John A. Oates, who had fallen out sick on the march. Colonel Oates had sent a horse for him. Finding him lying on the ground behind his company the colonel thought he was too ill to lead his men into the battle and told him so. However, the young Oates would have none of it. He was a man of pride, and these brothers were close. There was a time in the colonel's ruffian years when young John went from Alabama to Texas to coax his elder brother to come home and mend his ways. John got up off the ground and made ready to get into the fight.[65]

A last minute detail that needed attention was to send out a "water detail" for the regiment, tired and thirsty from the long march to the battlefield. Two men from each of Oates' 11 companies were selected to gather up the canteens of the men and head for a well located about 100 yards to the rear of their line, probably the Andrew Currens farm. But before the water detail could fill the canteens and return to the line, the advance was ordered. The water detail followed the expected line of advance but missed their regiment and walked right into the arms of Maj. Homer R. Stoughton's Second U.S. Sharpshooters, whose regiment had been sent out to cover Sickles' Third Corps left by Union General Ward. Adjutant Seymour F. Norton with about twelve of his sharpshooters corralled the 22 men from the water detail, canteens and all. Those men and their precious cargo would be sorely missed.[66]

Also, at the onset, five companies of Confederate skirmishers; one tenth of the brigade strength preceding General Law's line, (three from the 47th Alabama and two from the 48th Alabama), had been put out. Due to unclear orders or other confusion, these men marched

The Andrew Currens farmhouse today. It is believed that Oates' water detail came to a well near here to replenish the supply, for the men were thirsty and tired from their long march to the battlefield.

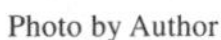

Photo by Author

out of the right, and continued marching — around the southern base of Big Round Top and out of the battle altogether! Colonel Oates later stated that Gen. Law had not told the regimental commanders of "what was intended to be done," before the advance began.[67]

"But a trammel"

Colonel James W. Jackson ordered his 47th Alabama forward, "Trail arms and quick time march!" But shortly after the first volley from Union sharpshooters felled a few of his men, confusion resulted and Col. Jackson was out of the fight. Disgraced at Gettysburg, he resigned his commission and went home shortly after the battle. It was later said that "the colonel remained so far behind that his presence on the field was but a trammel to the lieutenant-colonel."[68]

Colonel James W. Jackson has long been one of the enigmas of Gettysburg. He was born on September 28, 1831, making him 31 years old at the Battle of Gettysburg, young for a colonel in any war. His situation deserves a closer inspection, for he left the service under a cloud of suspicion for cowardice. Perhaps historians have been a little harsh in telling his Gettysburg tale and perhaps even more so by passing over it without much notice. For if the truth be known, he did his part.

Jackson had been very ill for much of the time, since he entered the Confederate service in February 1861, being absent sick about one third of the time. Prior to the War, he had been a doctor, receiving his training in New York City. He practiced in Georgia for a few years before settling in Lafayette, Alabama, where it is said he became "much attached to the people of that state." In the fall of 1860 Dr. Jackson, an avid secessionist, did his part and helped organize a company of men called the "Lafayette Guards." He was promptly elected captain. A year later, with the War already in progress, he raised another company. He was wounded at Sharpsburg (Antietam). At Gettysburg he was a full colonel in command of the 47th Alabama. It appears that he was well respected.

During May and June 1863, it seems his medical condition had much worsened, forcing him to resign his colonelcy on June 23, 1863. This resignation request was approved by Gen. Law, his immediate superior, on June 26, and followed by recommendations for approval by both Hood on June 28 and Longstreet the next day. Probably, he

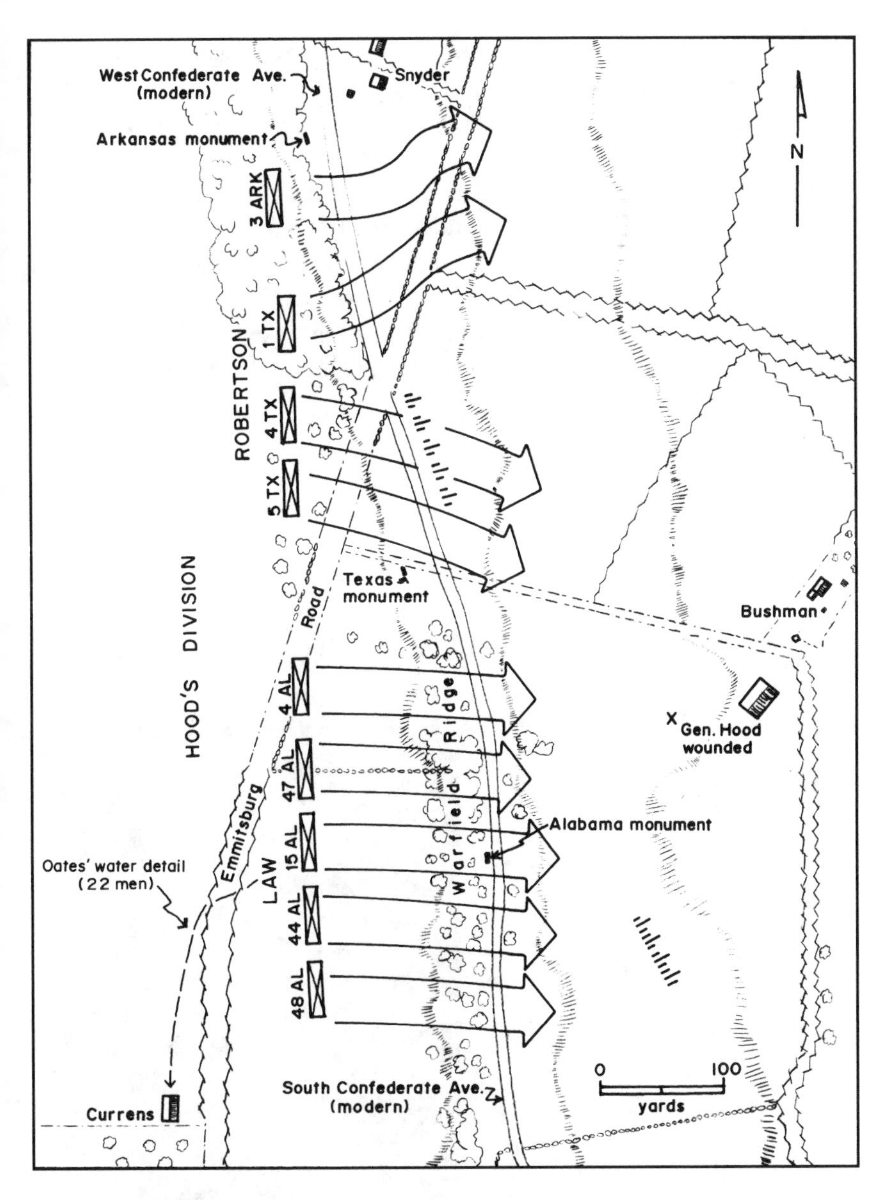

Approx. 4:00 p.m., Hood's Division, with brigades under Law and Robertson, steps off and the battle sequence starts from the Southern perspective. General Hood is wounded early in the fight. General Evander M. Law takes command. Colonel Oates' water detail is left behind, a fact that would later prove costly.

should not even have been on the field that day at Gettysburg, but administrative processing left his release from service in the air. That his resignation was approved on July 16, 1863, probably had more to do with time and circumstances of administration than his showing in the battle, but some among the ranks may have spoken otherwise. So Jackson returned home and never really recovered from his illness which was described by the attending physician as dyspepsia, an "irregular and painful action of the bowels." He gradually grew weaker and died on July 1, 1865, shortly after the end of the War. He left a widow, a five-year-old daughter and an infant boy nine months old. He was only 34 years old.[69]

Lt. Col. Michael J. Bulger

Soon after Col. James W. Jackson fell out, Lt. Leigh Terrell, one of Gen. Law's staff officers, rode up to Lt. Col. Michael J. Bulger and placed him in command of the regiment. Bulger, an ancient warrior at age 57, answered the call and boldly moved the regiment forward.[70]

Born on February 13, 1806, Lt. Col. Michael J. Bulger was enterprising. As a young man he had been a merchant, land owner, slave owner and a politician, and the fact that he made a comfortable living from his endeavors is evidence that what he chose to do he did well. As a state delegate, he attended the State Secession Convention and when the question of secession arose he vehemently opposed it, a courageous act in itself; being surrounded by a largely pro-secession body. Speaking in an oratory manner, Bulger told those present:

Alabama Dept. of Archives and History

Lt. Col. Michale J. Bulger, 47th Alabama

> When I have recorded my vote and protested against the passage of this ordinance, I will have conscientiously discharged my duty to those who sent me here, to my country and to my God. And when you have seceded this State and war comes, as it will come, the issue will be changed. And although I have advanced beyond the age of an ordinary soldier, I will be found in the front ranks of those who will go out to defend the rights of my section and the sovereignty of my State. Then, sire, if I see some of the valiant members who are going to whip the Yankees ten to one, and drink all the blood that will be spilled, I'll have to look behind me.

His address to the Convention summed up the man. In spite of his own beliefs, he would stick by the South and rally around its new flag. And when the storm of war rose, Bulger raised a regiment and got himself into the fray — he was a man of his word. Even though he was largely responsible for raising the regiment, he was not elected to command it. Instead, he was elected captain, probably due to his earlier anti-secession views.

While at the front during the Battle of Cedar Run, Va., on August 9, 1862, a Union bullet severed the artery in Capt. Bulger's right leg. Surgeons wanted to amputate. Bulger refused to allow them to do so, sought other medical aid more to his liking, and the leg was saved. Now, at Gettysburg, he would have to compensate for young Col. Jackson, who, whether ill, frightened, or otherwise removed from the position of leadership, left a void that needed filling. The 47th Alabama men continued to move forward under Lt. Col. Bulger's command.[71]

Crossing over down-sloping, then leveling terrain of rocks, plowed ground, bushes, trees and fences, Law's men and some of Robertson's Brigade passed the Bushman farmhouse, all the while being harassed by Smith's Union artillery battery from Devil's Den. In addition to pouring down a raking fire on the advancing Confederate line and also targeting Reilly's Confederate battery posted on the right of the Confederate advance line, Smith's artillerists got lucky. For no sooner had the Confederates begun the attack than Gen. John Bell Hood got taken out of it.

While advancing with his line, a shell exploded in the air above Gen. Hood, raining down fragments that cut through and shattered his left arm. He was borne from the field after turning command over to Gen. Evander M. Law. Hood would lose his arm as a result of this wound. The two left regiments of the Texas Brigade, the 1st Texas and 3rd Arkansas, broke away early in the advance and headed to Devil's Den to quiet Smith's guns. The Confederates also came under heavy fire from Union Col. Homer R. Stoughton's 2nd Regiment of U.S. Sharpshooters, who were covering General Ward's front as a skirmish line on the Union Third Corps left. Five companies of sharpshooters; companies D, E, H, B and F, were active in the effort to slow the Confederate advance through the areas of the Bushman and Slyder Farms in the approach to their objective, Little Round Top, or the valley between the Round Tops to locate and turn the Union left.[72]

The U.S. Sharpshooters

The Union sharpshooters were the brainchild of Col. Hiram Berdan. This was an elite group of hand picked marksmen comprising two regiments, the 1st and 2nd U.S. Sharpshooters, men from eight states, who each could at a distance of 200 yards "put 10 consecutive shots in a target, the average distance not to exceed five inches from the center of the bullseye." Colonel Berdan was at Gettysburg in command of the 1st Regiment, U.S. Sharpshooters, operating to the right of the action. The 2nd Regiment, specifically companies D, E, H, B and F under the command of Col. Homer R. Stoughton, were operating in the area covering the approach to the ravine between the Round Tops. In their distinctive green uniforms, they not only instilled fear in their opponents, but easily melted into the foliage on the battlefield. In addition, two men in each company had "climbers" to wear (metal spikes), that could help them climb into trees to give them a commanding view of the battlefield and bring any advancing foe into view at the earliest possible moment. Armed with the better Sharps rifle, a breechloading weapon with open sights, which could deliver a .52 caliber conical ball at high velocity, they were able to achieve devastating results at long range. And breechloading rifles could deliver ten shots per minute as opposed to three for muzzleloaders. The sharpshooters put up a mean resistance at the Bushman and Slyder farms, conducting a "fighting retreat;" giving up ground slowly while littering the battlefield with gray clad wrecks — bleeding, gasping, still.[73]

Trouble at Devil's Den!

Seeing that more help was needed on his left, Law directed his two right regiments, the 44th and 48th Alabama to drop back and turn left under cover of the 15th Alabama and 47th Alabama, and head for Devil's Den and Smith's guns. The 44th Alabama made the move first, the 48th following, establishing a second line. The shift took place just west of Plum Run; a small creek east of the Slyder farm. This placed the 47th and 15th Alabama on the right of the Confederate attack line.[74] Two of Robertson's regiments, the 5th and 4th Texas, continued forward in the attack with the 47th and the 15th Alabama, through the Slyder farm area. Oates later remembered:

> Gen. Law rode up to me as we were advancing and informed me that I was then on the extreme right of our line and for me to hug the base of Great Round Top and go up the valley between the two mountains, until I found the left of the Union line, to turn it and do all the damage I could and that Lt. Col. Bulger would be instructed to keep the 47th Alabama closed to my regiment, and if separated from he brigade he would act under my orders.[75]

Oates' Attack Stalled by Lt. Seymour F. Norton and Sharpshooters

Just as Oates' regiment was bearing left to converge with other regiments heading for the valley between the Round Tops, they crossed a small feeder branch of Plum Run, which ran perpendicular to the main stream. As the regiment crossed the brook, they received a galling first fire from the 2nd Regiment, U.S. Sharpshooters. Adjutant Seymour F. Norton and about a dozen of his men from Company B, positioned in the woods below Big Round Top, became the nemesis. From their position behind the stone wall, elevated some 40 feet above the gradually sloping ground and about 150 yards away, the sharpshooters opened fire into the flank and rear of the advancing Confederate soldiers and raised havoc in the ranks.

While the first fire on his right caught his attention, Oates did not get distracted from his goal — the ravine between the Round Tops and that golden opportunity on the Union left. But then Norton's sharpshooters poured a second volley into the flank of the 15th Ala-

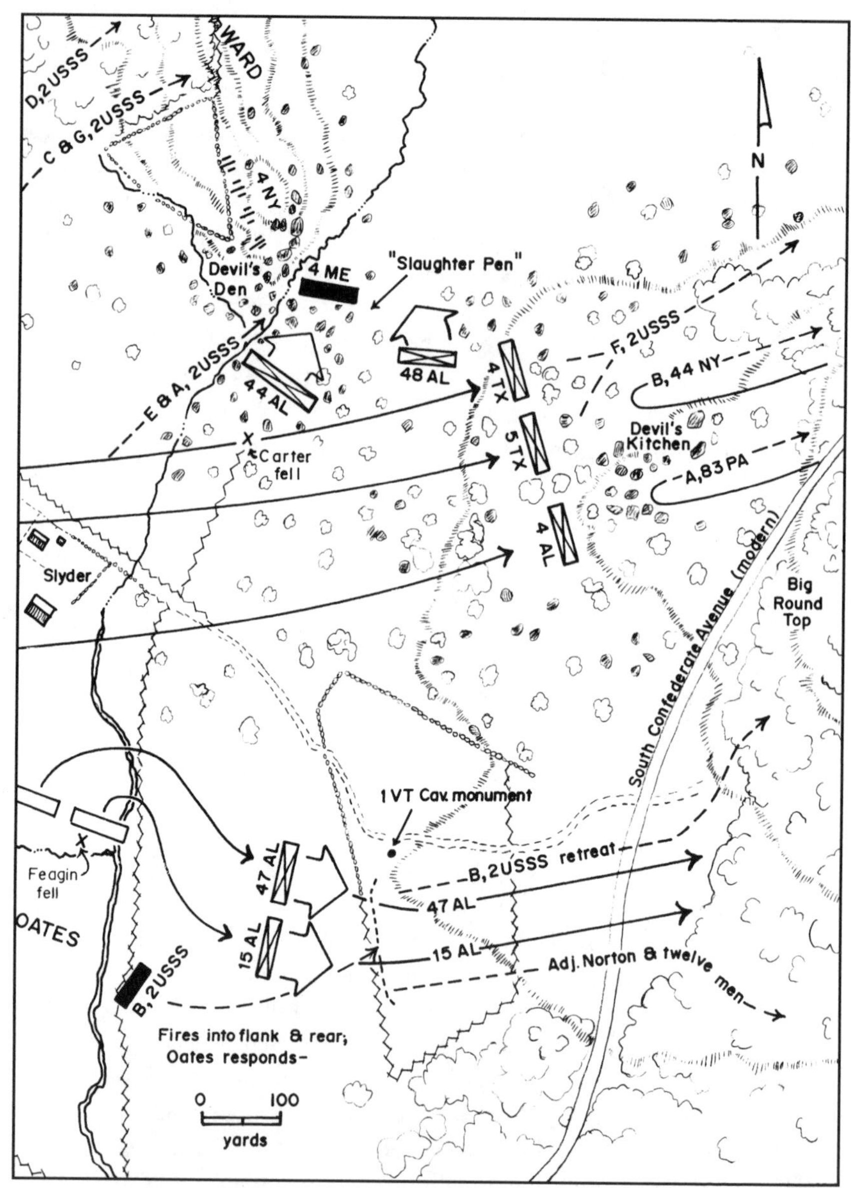

Approx. 4:30-5:15 p.m., as the 44th and 48th Alabama become engaged at Devil's Den, taking them out of the surge toward Little Round Top, the 4th and 5th Texas press forward with the 4th Alabama. Lt. Norton's small group of 12 to 15 Sharpshooters create havoc for the 15th Alabama by firing into its right flank and rear. Oates swings two regiments to the right, and out of the immediate thrust for Little Round Top to address the threat. First contact is made between Union and Confederate forces in the "Devil's Kitchen" as the 4th and 5th Texas and 4th Alabama turn the Union skirmishers back. Oates pushes up Big Round Top.

bama and Lt. Col. Isaac B. Feagin, Oates' second in command, went down, shot in the right knee while urging his men on. Feagin would be captured and lose his leg.

Lt. Col. Feagin's honor had been under a cloud of doubt ever since being charged with cowardice by Gen. D.H. Hill, for allegedly skulking behind some haystacks in the thick of battle at Antietam, in September 1862. But such was not the case. Feagin had actually gone to retrieve ammunition from the wounded men lying behind cover to replenish the dwindling supply of his hard fighting men on the line. General Hill, on the scene only momentarily, acted too hastily, without first obtaining the facts. Colonel Oates himself was the judge advocate of the court martial that tried him. Then Captain, Feagin was honorably acquitted and returned to duty. Soon afterward, about May 1, 1863, he was promoted to lieutenant colonel and placed at the head of the regiment. And as for Feagin's mettle at Gettysburg, Oates noted his gallantry on that field in his after-battle report.[76]

Seeing Lt. Col. Feagin and others fall, with a continual shower of lead balls coming from his right, Col. Oates acted to address the threat. The 47th Alabama followed his lead. "I gave the command to change direction to the right," Oates said. "The Forty-seventh Alabama, Lieutenant-colonel Bulger commanding, double-quicked around to keep in line with my regiment, and in doing so got telescoped into our left and the men were mixed several lines deep."[77]

Alabama Dept. of Archives and History

Lt. Col. Isaac B. Feagin, 15th Alabama

Sergeant William Holley, the file closer on Oates' left, trying to keep the line straight, yelled out to his colonel, "Colonel Oates, make Colonel Bulger take his damned concern out of our regiment!" But the crowding continued as soldiers hurried to catch up, adding to the confusion as they wheeled toward the right and across Plum Run, heading in a southeasterly direction toward the western base of Big Round Top. Certainly, the excitement was magnified as the sharpshooters continued to pour fire into the Confederate ranks. They could be seen darting from rock to tree, mostly shooting from cover positions, as they slowly retreated back and then up the side of Big Round Top, until they were about half way up the mountain. Then the sharpshooters split up, half vanishing into the woods to the north and the remainder melting into the foliage to the south side of the hill, all the while gaining precious time for the Union cause. Oates later wrote that their sudden departure was "as though commanded by a magician."

But Oates had not seen the last of the sharpshooters. Many would just as "magically" reappear to cause him further grief later on. Oates, however, continued to press on up Big Round Top until some of his men fainted from exhaustion and lack of water. He knew they could not go on, and he ordered his men to halt near the summit.[78]

Unbeknownst to Col. Oates, the portion of 2nd Sharpshooters disappearing to the right was undoubtedly Lt. Norton with his dozen or so men from Company B. They probably remained in the area for awhile and there corralled the 22 men from Oates' "water detail," who would have been trying to catch up with their regiment. Being heavily laden, each man carrying several filled canteens for their respective companies, they made an easy mark for the sharpshooters.

As a result of the actions of Norton and his small squad of sharpshooters, the Confederate attack force was effectively split at a critical time in the battle. This would have serious consequences, contributing toward the Confederate defeat at Little Round Top.

If the first hero of Little Round Top was General G. K. Warren, for recognizing the importance of the hill and his effort to have it defended, and the second, and central hero of the battle was Col. Strong Vincent, for taking his Fifth Corps brigade up to the summit before orders to do so could be formulated by his superiors, then third honors, even before Col. O'Rorke and Col. Chamberlain could cover themselves in glory that day, might have to go to the little-known Adjutant of the 2nd U.S. Sharpshooters, Lt. Seymour F. Norton, who never made it to Little Round Top at all! Adjutant Norton and his 12 men from Co. B, were not only instrumental in capturing Col. Oates' 22 men from the water detail. More importantly, it was Norton and his men who caused two whole regiments, the 15th and 47th Alabama, to be diverted from the course of their advance. Otherwise, they would have struck simultaneously with the 4th Alabama, 5th and 4th Texas regiments — in one thrusting, crushing blow, to possibly break the Union line.

National Archives

Lt. Seymour F. Norton
Co. B, Second U.S. Sharpshooters

Norton and his men, with their popping and peppering of the flank and rear of the 15th and 47th Alabama from their position near the western base of Big Round Top, caused Col. Oates (not knowing the actual size of Norton's force), to wheel two full regiments to the right to meet the threat, taking them out of the initial attack thrust. They became like another attack force all their own, another prong, and it operated independent of the other three regiments, thereby lessening the effectiveness of the entire brigade.

Some 25 years after Gettysburg, in a complimentary letter to Col. H. R. Stoughton by Col. William C. Oates, the fact that Lt. Norton and his men were able to divert two full regiments away from the main attack force, was called key to the Union victory. (See "Little Round Top Talk" for Oates' Nov. 22, 1888 letter to Maj. Stoughton in its entirety).[79]

Texans Having Tough Time — 4th Alabamians too!

Meanwhile, on the brigade left, the 5th and 4th Texas and the 4th Alabama were having troubles of their own. Having been first harassed by Stoughton's Sharpshooters from Co. D northeast of the Bushman farm, they next ran into a real hornets nest when they came up against no less than four companies of Stoughton's men, Co.'s A,

E, F and H to be exact, at the William Slyder farm, a two story log house with barn and a number of sheds surrounded by post rail fences and stone walls. "Men were falling, stricken to death," said one member of the 4th Alabama.[80]

Major Stoughton in his report stated, "While they (the Rebels) were advancing the Second Regiment (of U.S. Sharpshooters) did splendid execution, killing and wounding a great many. One regiment broke three times and rallied before it would advance."[81]

Photo by Author

The Slyder Farm today.

The Alabamians went to the bayonet to carry the farm grounds with the Sharpshooters retreating in small squads or detachments, some toward Devil's Den, others east toward Devil's Kitchen, another grotesque boulder field below the Round Tops.[82]

As the Confederates passed through the Slyder Farm area, they splashed through Plum Run and into the woods finding the Sharpshooters again behind another stone wall. As the Confederates approached, the Sharpshooters renewed their vigor, firing and retreating, the classic "fighting retreat," for which they were well trained, each time moving to cover, minimizing their potential to be hit as compared to the more exposed movements of the Confederate infantry on the field.

Col. R. M. Powell & Lt. Col. B.F. Carter

Colonel Robert M. Powell, 5th Texas, reached the wall yelling "Forward!" to his men, jumped the wall, met no opposition, and angled left across the wooded shoulder of the hill. Lt. Col. Benjamin F. Carter of the 4th Texas would not be so lucky. In the area of the stone wall, an artillery shell crashed near him and Carter was hit in the face and both legs by a barrage of rock and fragments. He lay there mortally wounded and sometime afterward was captured. He would die in a Union hospital in Chambersburg on July 21.[83]

A frail man by military standards, he even needed help in having his equipment carried by others. Yet Carter was one of the most beloved officers in the Texas brigade. He was remembered by one Texas soldier as having "no superior intellectually in the Regiment, but also had a gift of knowing how to explain every set down in "Hardee's Tactics" so thoroughly that the biggest blockhead in the ranks could understand."[84]

Lieutenant Colonel Benjamin F. Carter was certainly an extraordinary man. Before going off to war he had been a lawyer with a thriving practice in Austin, Texas. There, he met and married the daughter of William Rust, Austin's postmaster, and was active in lo-

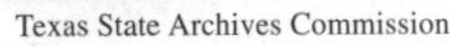

Texas State Archives Commission

***Col. Robert M. Powell,*
*5th Texas***

Austin History Center, Austin, Texas

***Lt. Col. Benjamin F. Carter,*
*4th Texas***

cal politics, serving on the Austin City Council in 1857, before being elected mayor of Austin in 1857 at the age of 27. Austin was a booming young city of just over 10,000 people, of which about 39% were black slaves.[85]

During this period Lt. Col. Carter and his wife, Louisa, had three lovely daughters born to them. Then the war came along and ruined everything for families both North and South, but it seems that the Carters got more than their share of the grief.

Though universally loved by the men, Lt. Col. Carter was a bit squeamish about visiting the sick. When in "Camp Texas" just outside of Richmond early in the war, many Texans came down with typhoid fever, exposure and other illnesses. Hundreds died before they ever got to see the enemy. Though Carter never visited the men, he sent other soldiers to check on them and see to their needs, often sending along treats paid for out of his own pocket. He explained that he "could not bear to see anyone suffer," and that he had "a perfect horror of the sick room." This horror was probably magnified the day the Devil scratched at his own door, when he received news from Austin that his wife and two of his daughters had died due to illness. His only surviving child, Ella, was left in the care of relatives.

Further proof of Lt. Col. Carter's appeal is the fact that even though absent from Austin for two years, he was elected to the bench of the 2nd District Court in Texas, on August 3, 1863, before word of his wounding and subsequent death reached home. He was only 32 years old at Gettysburg.[86]

In about the same area of the battlefield where Lt. Col. Benjamin F. Carter met disaster, another officer made a bad mistake. This was Lt. Joe Smith of Co. E, 4th Texas. While crossing Plum Run, Smith doused his handkerchief in the water and tied it around his head to beat the scorching heat. It must have attracted the attention of Union sharpshooters, for moments later a hail of Union bullets found their mark and the lieutenant was shot through the head several times. Eleven holes were later counted in the handkerchief — a sorry play in the game of chance.[87]

Private John C. West, also of Co. E, did not have to be at Gettysburg or in the War. As a district attorney in Waco, Texas, he was exempt by Confederate law from having to fight. But he thought it was his duty to serve, so he joined the Army. He sought no command or commission, as others of his station normally did, but instead took his place on the line as a private soldier, fighting for the Confederacy. And as he watched the advancing troops of his Texas brigade darting among the rocks, trees, and boulders on the battlefield at Gettysburg, he could not help but think of the alliteration, "Round the rude rock the ragged rascal ran." Just then, a bullet went through his beard and ricocheted off a rock near his head, a fragment cutting his lip. But the literate West was lucky; he would live to write about his war experiences and lead a long and productive life as a judge and fill other positions of public service back home in Waco.[88]

Through the woods the Confederates continued to press, touching the northwest base of Big Round Top, and continuing through the Devil's Kitchen area. Ancient Indian rituals were thought to have occurred there. It was a forbidding place, as it is today, with large granite boulders of all sizes and shapes piled upon each other in grotesque array. In this area, Union skirmishers from the 83rd Pennsylvania and the 44th New York regiments, having pushed out about 200 yards from the slopes of Little Round Top, came upon their foe. The first contact shots of the battle for Little Round Top proper, were probably fired in these woods.

Oates Hesitates, A Precious Moment Lost

From the summit of Big Round Top, Oates was astonished to find that he could see the whole battlefield through the trees before him. He could see the death grapple in Devil's Den, battle smoke hanging over the Wheatfield and hear the roar of artillery and musketry along the battle lines. He imagined what a battery could do if deployed on Big Round Top. Within five minutes, Capt. Leigh R. Terrell, Assistant Adjutant to Gen. Law rode up the hill from the only pathway accessible, on the southeast side of Big Round Top. Terrell wanted to know why Oates had stopped. Oates described his weary, worn and thirsty men and then drew attention to his present position, saying that it was the best on the battlefield and what damage he thought a few good artillery pieces could do from its summit. "Within a half hour," Oates later wrote, "I could convert it (Big Round Top), into a Gibraltar that I could hold against ten times the number of men I had…" But Capt. Terrell would not listen. He told Col. Oates that General Hood was wounded, General Law was now in command of the division, and the general expected Oates to carry out his orders to turn the Union left as originally planned. Oates did not argue. Terrell left and Oates put his men into motion again.[89]

Oates ordered both regiments to face to the left and moved by the left flank to avoid a large precipice of rocks to his front — boulders of enormous size — and then completed a tricky movement, ordering the line by the right flank forward swinging into a left oblique on down the hill. A pretty sight, it could probably only have been done effectively by seasoned, well trained troops. And as they proceeded to descend the mountain, Oates could see, "in plain view, the Federal wagon-trains and less than 300 yards distant an extensive park of ordnance wagons..." Exactly how many wagons there were no one knows, and over time the number must have grown in Oates' mind. But it is probable that the wagons that Col. Oates did see were the ordnance wagons of the 24-year-old West Point artillerist, Lt. Charles Hazlett's Battery D, 5th U.S. Artillery, which would soon be playing havoc with Confederates from the summit of Little Round Top. In any event, it was clear to Oates that he had found the Union left, ripe for the picking. He quickly dispatched Co. A of the 15th Alabama under Capt. Francis K. Shaaf, to surround and capture the wagons. Shaaf and his men broke to the right and out of sight. Through the trees, clear of underbrush, Oates soon could see the Federals' splendid line of breastworks — and Union troops waiting. He was about ten minutes too late from getting there first. Down upon the saddle between the Round Tops they swept, in a clash of wills, minds, and ideologies.[90]

Rumblings Before The Storm

Whether the Union's 16th Michigan skirmishers went out on the left or the right, it is apparent that somehow some of them made it to Big Round Top, for the young 22-year-old adjutant of the 16th Michigan, Lt. Rufus. W. Jacklin, remembered "firing the first shots down upon their advance column from the Big Round Top…," and that it "was the signal of attack." But he says nothing of what happened next. It is likely that most of the men of the 16th who had ventured out as skirmishers ran into the green clad retreating 2nd Regiment U.S. Sharpshooters who had come over Big Round Top with news that the enemy was not far behind. Colonel Oates' ascent, pause, and renewed advance must have eaten up twenty or so minutes of precious time — time enough for the Michiganders to do some damage to the initial Confederate thrust in the ravine below, between the Round Tops before heading back.

Michigan State Archives

Lt. Rufus W. Jacklin, 16th Michigan.

It is possible that some of the Michigan skirmishers fell in with Capt. Morrill's Co. B of the 20th Maine, who took a position by the stone wall on the far left of the Union line. But Morrill never mentioned them in his after action report. Most of them probably retreated between Morrill's skirmish line and the 20th Maine regiment, finding their way to the rear of that regiment and then moving under cover behind the lines until they found their own regiment on the far right. However, the return of those two companies of skirmishers from the 16th Michigan was never recorded in any report nor otherwise illuminated by the pen of any veteran afterward.[91]

"Goodbye Billy!"

Sometimes the unexplainable occurs. Such was the case of Capt. Lucius S. Larrabee of the 44th New York Regiment, who had a premonition that the next battle would be his last. "Since our last battle," Larrabee said, "I have known that I would be killed the next time I was under fire." While other officers of the regiment tried to cheer him up, he took his watch and valuables and together with the address of his brother in Chicago, gave them to the 44th's Quartermaster Mundy for safekeeping. As he went forward in command of the 44th New York Co. B skirmish line, he bid farewell to Capt. William R. Bourne saying, "Good bye Billy, I shall never see you again," and went down the slope to "feel" for the Confederate advance.[92]

First contact was made about 200 yards to the front in the area of Devil's Kitchen, with the 4th Alabama, and 5th and 4th Texas regiments advancing, with each step forcing the skirmishers back. Larrabee, upon initially seeing the enemy a short distance away, advancing in two or more lines of battle, wisely ordered the retreat of his skirmishers. While executing this movement, however, Capt. Larrabee was shot through the body, instantly killed at the first volley. His premonition had come true.[93]

The Devil's Carnival, Approx. 5:15 p.m.

Through the clearing between the Round Tops they came. With their Rebel yells and loud demonstration, they started up the slope of that craggy rise. As soon as the Union skirmishers could get back in, the Union line opened with a blaze of seething fire into the ranks of what had become the left prong of the now disjoined Confederate attack. Fully in anticipation of what was to come, the butternut boys got off a volley of their own, so as to make the first fire almost simultaneous.[94]

"A long line of us went down, three of us close together," Pvt. W. C. Ward, later wrote. "There was a sharp, electric pain in the lower part of the body, and then a sinking sensation to the earth: and, falling, all things growing dark, the one and last idea passing through the mind was: 'This is the last of earth.'" Ward had been hit. "Minie balls were falling through leaves like hail in a thunderstorm." When consciousness returned, Ward dragged himself to the cover of a large boulder until he could be borne off the field.[95]

The south side of the mountain lit up like an inferno, as the battle opened against the center and right of the Union line. The Southerners tried to wrest from the Union troops there ensconced — the prize — the very jewel of Gettysburg — Little Round Top!

Captain John S. Cleveland of the 5th Texas offered a purse to the first of his comrades over the works. Sergeant Ross sprang forward to be the first to try, but his Captain ordered him back, saying, "File closers not included." Then, Col. R. M. Powell shouted "Swing up left, Major Rogers." "I'll do it, Colonel, by jingo!" said Rogers. It was a weird moment, for as Rogers was about to say the words, "by jingo!" a momentary hush had come over the battlefield and his words rang out, clear and distinct, sounding so ludicrous that some of the men began to laugh. To Col. Powell, the affair took on a surreal form, as he later wrote, "The scene was strikingly like a devil's carnival. Another yell and desperate charge followed, succumbed by a sudden and awful hush, just as if every one had been stricken instantly with death." Surely, it was no laughing matter.[96]

Col. Vincent Excels!

Quickly assessing the situation on the hill, Col. Vincent turned to his adjutant, Lt. John Clark and said, "Go and tell General Barnes to send me reinforcements at once; the enemy are coming against us with an overwhelming force." Then, he jumped up on top of a large rock to get a better view. The butternut boys were coming in swarms as the volume of fire increased. The colonel knew that every second counted and could mean the difference between success and failure.[97]

Vincent could be seen everywhere up and down the line, encouraging his men. As the rage of fire reached a fever pitch, his men took on the form of a scowling giant, awakened from sleep, breathing fire down on the advancing foe, now licking, then hissing between the trees, enveloping the rocks below. Through the thickening haze of battle smoke, the figures moved, reaching, pushing, pressing forward and back, as the shifting battle line swayed in a clash of wills.

As the battle developed, it extended toward the Union left. The right of the 20th Maine became hotly engaged before its skirmish line could return. Failure to return could only point to their being cut off, captured, or worse. Too bad, Capt. Walter G. Morrill was a fine leader. Those 50 men of Company B would be sorely missed![98]

Early in the fight, there was a gap of approximately 200 ft., between the left of the 83rd Pennsylvania and the 20th Maine. This was probably due to the bow shaped line of the 83rd Pennsylvania, which in following the contour of the hill bent slightly forward of the brigade line. Grasping at the opportunity, the 47th Alabama surged forward, Lt. Col. Bulger jumping onto a rock waving his sword in his left hand and encouraging his men. It was probably at this time that he was struck by a ball, which entered the left side of his chest and passed directly through the lung and lodged in his back. He slumped back down onto the ground and leaned against a tree behind the cover of the rock, bleeding profusely from the chest, mouth and nose. Bulger's men, too, found disaster instead of that opening in the Union line, for the fire from the blue line increased as the left companies of the 83rd Pennsylvania, from their bent forward position, pivoted toward the left and poured a stunning oblique fire into the front and left flank of the advancing 47th Alabama. And the billows of smoke, shower of lead and wind swept the Alabamians back to where they came from, minus a good part of their fighting force and their colonel. Though they would continue in the fight, they would not be able to muster the necessary punch to penetrate the Union line on Little Round Top. Things were beginning to look gloomy.[99]

On the left of the 47th Alabama came the men of the 4th Alabama under command of Lt. Col. Lawrence H. Scruggs, a cotton merchant from Huntsville. He had risen in the ranks from private to command the regiment at age 27 on the field at Gettysburg. Muscling back the Union sharpshooters through the farm fields in the approach to Little Round Top, even clashing with bayonets at one point at the stone fence near the Slyder Farm, the men of the 4th Alabama made their first rush against the blue line their best effort of the day. All they could do against the 83rd Pennsylvania and 44th New York was expend their ammunition before they were ordered to withdraw. "Owing to the exhausted condition of the men and the roughness of the mountain-side, we found it impossible to carry this position," Scruggs later reported. But coordination between Confederate regiments was also lacking, making cooperation between them almost impossible. And it showed.[100]

Col. Chamberlain On The Left

Chamberlain's attention was then drawn to a large force of Confederates trying to sweep around to gain his left. At Lt. James Nichols' urgings, Chamberlain mounted a large rock and observed "thick groups of gray," moving toward his flank. It was Oates' 15th Alabama boys, worn with marching and thirst, but hungry for the Union blue.[101]

Chamberlain had an intuitive grasp that lent to "innovation" at a moment of need. He formulated a plan to bend back or "refuse" his line to further protect his left. He summoned his company officers and ordered that the regiment maintain a hot fire in front "without special regard to its need or immediate effect." While trying to keep close to the 83rd Pennsylvania, the men were to side-step to the left, gradually coming into one rank.

At the extreme left of the front line was a large boulder where Chamberlain placed the regimental colors and there bent back the line at a right angle — doubling the original length of the line. It was done in clock-work fashion and masked well under the continuous fire of his regiment. He now awaited another attack by Oates' Alabamians in this new formation.[102]

Captain Orpheus S. Woodward, of the 83rd Pennsylvania, did his best to accommodate the movement of the 20th Maine. While he could not give Col. Chamberlain a full company of men as support, he did pull back the center of his line some ten or fifteen paces, straightening his front and extending it to the left to help close that dangerous gap. Chamberlain's right moved in conformity also and the door was shut.[103]

On they came, again in a rush, this time Oates' 15th Alabama men. They knew that these were times that test men's souls and purpose. Chamberlain's former training in rhetoric and theology excited his intuitive mind, and his perception of the scene took on images of the unimaginable, even the surreal. Men dropped around him, in front and behind. Men called out in anger, defiance, in pain and in fear. And always the musket roll — the volley, the peppering, and crackling of rifle fire, exiting the muzzle of a gun, hitting, a tree, a rock, or the deafening thud of a ball smashing into human flesh. The sounds of ramrods shoving another cartridge down a barrel, reloading as fast as they could to send another death messenger — looking for a home. And the distant sound of artillery, letting them know that there were other fights on this battlefield raging.

MOLLUS

Capt. Orpheus S. Woodward, 83rd Pennsylvania.

In front of Chamberlain's Co. H position on his left, Sgt. Isaac Lanthrop caught a musket ball in his stomach. He would die the next day. First Sergeant Charlie Steele, too, was hit. He staggered over to Capt. Land with a gaping chest wound. "My God, Sergeant Steele!" exclaimed Land as he saw the look of horror on the dying sergeant's face. "I am going, Captain!" said Steele, and he shortly fell in a crumpled mass.[104]

Colonel Oates thought that his Alabamians had penetrated the Maine defense five times throughout the battle, but each time they were thrown back. Chamberlain could be seen urging his men on at each step. At one point during the struggle, one member of the 15th Alabama placed his rifle securely on a boulder and found Chamberlain in his sights. But as he started to squeeze the trigger, a queer notion compelled him to stop. After going through these motions again and failing still, he gave it up and moved on to other quarry, sparing the colonel's life.[105] (See "Little Round Top Talk" for more complete details, under "I Had You Perfectly Certain").

For an hour more the pulsing thrusts continued all along the line of the 83rd Pennsylvania, 44th New York and 16th Michigan as well. Each time the Rebels were repelled and they withdrew back down the slope.

During one assault, Lt. Eugene L. Dunham of the 44th New York was shot dead in the head while encouraging his men. Here, Vincent's Brigade found themselves trading shots with the 4th Alabama and the 4th and 5th Texas regiments. The 16th Michigan, smallest of the Union regiments on the hill, began to feel the pressure of hot Texas lead as the Texans tried to find a way to flank Welch's Regiment, which was hanging "in the air," exposed.[106]

It was worse on the Confederate side. The 5th Texas color-bearer, T. W. Fitzgerald, of Co. A, was badly wounded near the front. Captain J. A. Howard of Co. B picked up the standard and was almost instantly killed. Sergeant W. S. Evans of Co. F got angry, planted the colors defiantly in the face of the enemy, and survived. There was death and destruction all around.[107]

With bullets whizzing around them so thickly that it seemed "a man could hold out a hat and catch it full," the men of Co. K, 5th Texas, worked their way to within about 20 yards of the Union line when their advance began to stall. Twin brothers from Co. C who were inseparable, somehow got into Co. K's line. A bullet hit one brother and as the other helped him to the ground, another bullet got him as well. Another mother back home in the Lone Star State felt

Texas State Archives Commission

Lt. Col. King Bryan, 5th Texas.

the agony of war as two souls lifted from the hill where her sons' bodies lay still. The blue-gray smoke thickened — death's shadow — each time a trigger was pulled.[108]

Seeing that his men could not advance without reinforcements, Lt. Col. King Bryan went in search of Col. Robert M. Powell, to find out what to do next. Moving through dead bodies and broken men he feared the worst for his colonel. "I had not proceeded far," said Bryan, "when I discovered the prostrate form of our noble colonel, who had fallen at his post, his face to the foe." Hurrying toward the colonel, Bryan himself was struck in the left arm. "On reaching the colonel, I found that he was not dead; but seeing the rent in his coat where the ball passed out, my fears were excited that his wound would prove mortal. The hemorrhage from my own wound forced me from the field, leaving the command to Major [Jefferson C.] Rogers."[109]

Powell was seriously wounded in the chest, shot clear through, and could not be safely moved. Bryan made it back to the rear and medical attention as the Texans again fell back down the slope where Maj. Rogers reformed his men to lead another spirited attack back up the hill in one last desperate attempt to break the Union line.[110]

"Paddy, Give Me A Regiment!

While all this was going on, Gen. Gouverneur K. Warren, unaware of the presence of Vincent's Brigade on Little Round Top, was trying to get troops up on the hill. With his aide, Lt. Washington Roebling, Warren raced down the northern base of the hill and spied Gen. Weed's Brigade heading to support Gen. Sickles' Third Corps at the Wheatfield. Weed had gone ahead to make dispositions for placement of his brigade, caused Warren to find Col. Patrick O'Rorke at the front of the brigade. Warren knew O'Rorke well from West Point days when Warren was an instructor and young O'Rorke was a bright student. Riding up Warren shouted, "Paddy, give me a regiment!" O'Rorke answered that Gen. Weed had gone ahead and was expecting the brigade to follow him. Warren replied, "Never mind that, bring your regiment up here and I will take the responsibility." O'Rorke obeyed, taking his own regiment up the hill and allowing other troops of the brigade to continue on to Gen. Weed. Lieutenant Roebling led the way as Gen. Warren went to confer with Fifth Corps Commander, Gen. Sykes about more support.[111]

Trouble On The Union Right!

Meanwhile, up on Little Round Top, the Union right was crumbling. The 16th Michigan with its paltry numbers could not withstand the pressure applied by the advancing 4th and 5th Texas, who were trying to turn Vincent's Brigade right. This time, however, the Texans were assisted by the 48th Alabama, who had pushed their way through Devil's Den in the valley below. The 48th Alabama men started climbing in a southeasterly direction, impacting directly on the right three companies of the 16th Michigan.

U.S. Military History Institute

Capt. Benjamin F. Partridge, 16th Michigan.

Captain Benjamin F. Partridge, hit twice during the battle, said, "I thought of nothing but my line of duty. Lt. Col. Norval E. Welch stood with the regt. Colors on a flat rock near the centre of the regt. Till it was not possible to remain longer in that place. The flag had several holes through it. I was immediately in his front and several shells burst near us throwing rocks everywhere." And Lt. Edward Hill said, "Every man of the color guard, save one, was killed. The colors, as if in pitying sympathy with their brave defenders, fell, shot from the staff, enveloping the fallen with their silken folds like a funeral pall." Each time the colors went down straining arms lifted them up again, but the added pressure of yet larger numbers of Confederates seemingly coming from all angles took its toll.[112]

Then, the onrush of Texans and Alabamians began to turn the right of the 16th Michigan as three of its companies began to falter, step back and stumble. In the confusion of battle and possibly sheer panic, Lt. William Kydd of Co. G, in an "entirely unwarrantable assumption of authority," gave the order to pull back the line of the 16th. Perhaps this was done in order to attempt to "refuse" the line, or to check the latest Confederate thrust. But the order through the smoke and din of battle was misunderstood and was construed instead as a retreat. About 45 men fell back with the colors and the colonel, clearly one third of the Michigan men in line, back behind the rocks in the rear of the 44th New York, as the battle became a fierce hand-to-hand and bayonet contest. Welch, in his after battle report said in connection with this movement that "someone (Gen. Weed or Gen. Sykes) called from the extreme crest of the hill to fall back nearer the top, where a much less exposed line could be taken up." But neither Sykes nor Weed was on Little Round Top at that time. In any case, this was a crushing blow to the Union right at Little Round Top, as the Alabamians and Texans started to climb over the hastily thrown up breastworks and mix bayonet thrusts and close range fire with the Michiganders who had stayed to fight. Captain Robert T. Elliott stepped up to command replacing Col. Welch who had vanished among the rocks to the rear. Elliott did his best to encourage the men, but his diminished numbers made his task nearly impossible.[113]

Michigan State Archives

Capt. Robert T. Elliott, 16th Michigan.

"Don't give an inch!"

When the fire of the fight was at its hottest, Col. Vincent mounted a large boulder on the hill behind the lines of the 44th New York, and the 16th Michigan line, to better direct the defense of the hill. There he could be seen urging his men on. By now, even the regimental drummers had dropped their sticks and picked up muskets to defend themselves. Vincent could see the right of his line exposed, vulnerable and crumbling, and through the battle smoke, the latest and strongest onrush of Confederate forces to press on that part of the field. He jumped off the rock and started making his way to that critical point. He would not get far. Quickly, Col. Vincent came upon Sgt. Charles E. Sprague of the 44th New York, who had sustained a serious gunshot wound in the left shoulder and was making for the rear. Sprague, bleeding profusely, had come upon the jumbled mass and was exhorting the Michiganders there to stand and fight like the men on the line of the 44th to their left. Sprague later recalled seeing Col. Vincent coming up on foot with his wife's riding crop in his hand, saying, "That will do, Sergeant Sprague; I'll take hold of this," and then Vincent went to driving the men of the16th back into line with his little whip as the sergeant started again for the rear and medical aid.[114]

The men of the 44th New York tried to provide support for the 16th Michigan by spinning on their heels and pouring a thunderous right oblique fire into the ranks of the oncoming Texans and Alabamians, where men were falling in clumps as the smoke thickened. Vincent continued his urgings, "Don't give an inch boys! Don't give an inch!" as he strained every nerve to put fire back into his men. But the Rebels were right in the mix and it was at about that time that Col. Vincent was hit with a ball, crashing into his left side, through the groin, and lodging into his right side. There he fell mortally wounded on the field. "This is the fourth or fifth time they have shot at me," he exclaimed, "and they have hit me at last!" He was immediately carried back to his original position near another boulder, this one located behind the 44th New York, where he had been directing the actions of the brigade, (probably the spot where today a small marker erroneously identifies the place of his wounding). There he remained until the fighting subsided and was then carried to the rear.

Vincent Marker — one of the first markers placed on the battlefield of Gettysburg, other than those in the National Cemetery. Marks the "supposed" site where Col. Vincent fell in battle. It more accurately marks the location of Vincent's Brigade headquarters where he directed operations during the battle. It is worth the short walk down the southern slope of Little Round Top to see.

Photo by Author

This spot might best be called Vincent's regimental headquarters position at the onset of the battle.[115]

When the fighting had opened, Col. Vincent's bugler Pvt. Oliver W. Norton left his horse and flag with the servants of the mounted officers, to pick up a musket and find a place on the right of the 44th New York line, to give the Rebels hell. Now his beloved commander was down. Surely, there was more than fire in his eyes.[116]

"Down this way boys!"

Colonel O'Rorke and his 140th New York Regiment wasted no time scaling the northwest side of the hill. General Warren had made himself clear. Union reinforcements were needed fast. But as they climbed the hill, they did not hear the sounds of immediate rifle exchange. "It was a strange thing," Lt. Porter Farley would later comment, "but it is a fact that we heard only canon, and the sounds as if very distant…we could not hear reports of musketry."[117] They probably experienced a phenomenon known as acoustic shadowing, whereby sound is deflected from its expected path due to atmospheric or physical conditions. As a result, they did not stop to load their weapons and went into the battle with empty guns. And as they

Courtesy Michael Albanese Collection
Col. Patrick H. O'Rorke, 140th New York.

Courtesy Michael Albanese Collection
Lt. Porter Farley, 140th New York.

climbed the hill diagonally from the northwest slope, Lt. Charles Hazlett's Co. D, 5th U.S. Artillery guns came pouring through the lines also headed for the summit on orders to support the Union troops on the left.[118] The rough terrain made it almost impossible for Hazlett to get the guns up. But horses straining to pull, soldiers struggling to push, and even a hand from Gen. Warren, then riding back up the hill, was enough to get them up and in place.[119]

However, before those guns could fire, Col. O'Rorke and his regiment of 526 officers and men, one of the largest in Gen. Weed's Brigade reached the summit in the nick of time. The crumbling right of the 16th Michigan was readily apparent as Confederate troops came swarming up to the line. Quickly dismounting his horse, young Col. Patrick O'Rorke drew his sword and gave the unmilitary order, "Down this way, boys!" The men of Companies A and G were nearest O'Rorke, and followed on his heels. And there, by the sheer weight of their bodies, they absorbed the shock of the first Confederate volley that ripped through their advancing line and dropped several men at each step, but not before being pushed from the summit of Little Round Top themselves. In the sheet of flame, O'Rorke was shot clear through the neck and there he fell, dead among the rocks without a sound.[120]

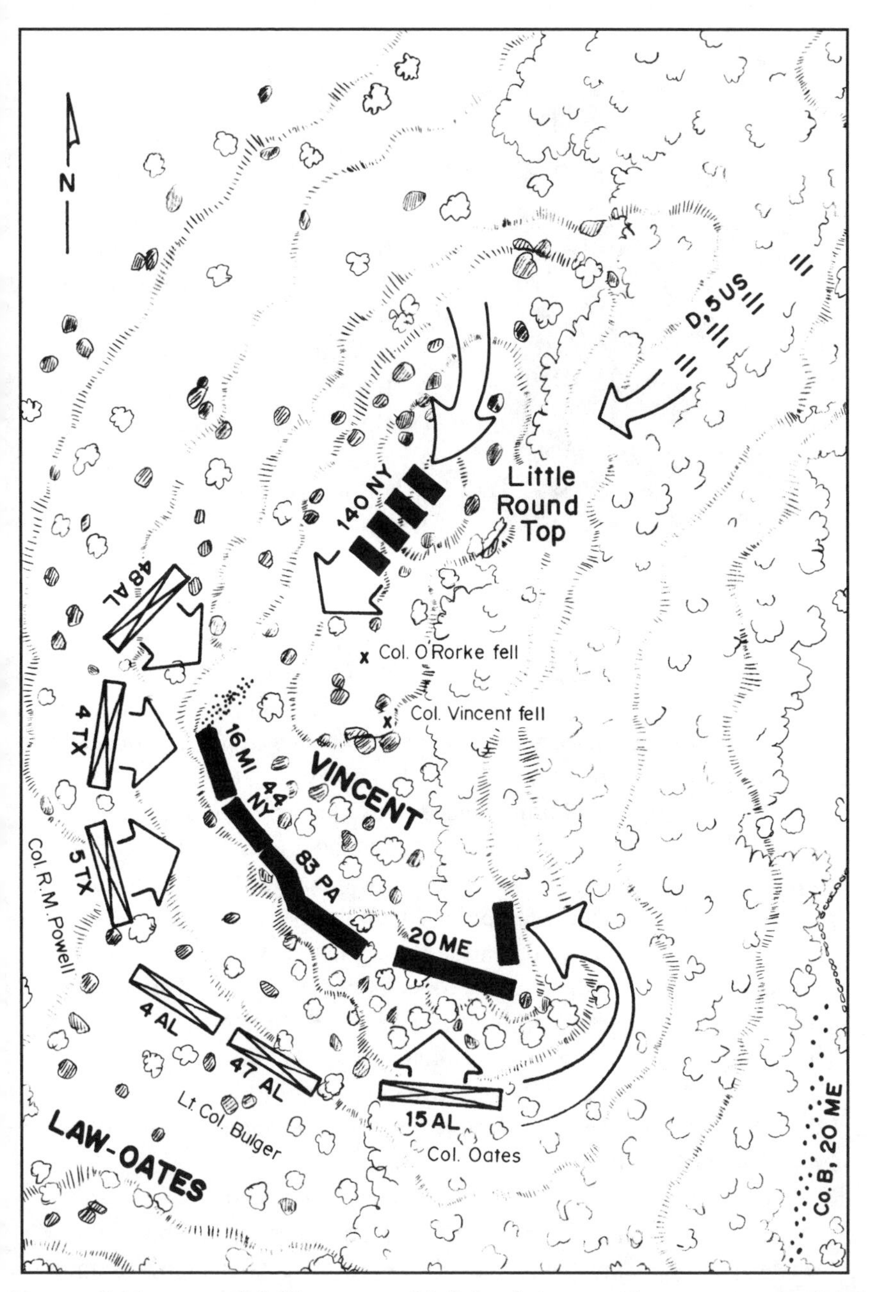

Approx. 5:15 p.m. — Col. Vincent gets his brigade into position ten minutes ahead of onrushing Confederate forces. Chamberlain sends out Capt. Walter G. Morrill and his Co. B to guard his left. O'Rorke's 140th New York arrives on the hill in the nick of time to stave off a Confederate breach on the Union right, and Lt. Charles Hazlett brings up his battery. The 15th Alabama surges around in an attempt to turn the Union left.

Courtesy Benedict Maryniak

Capt. Milo Starks, 140th New York.

The charging men continued past their fallen colonel and drove into the breach of the torn and breaking Michigan line. Captain Milo Starks and 1st Sgt. Charles Taylor of Co. A were at the head of the jumbled column. Taylor emerged unscathed, but Starks was wounded four times, twice in the right arm and once in his left hand and right leg. Despite his injuries, Starks stayed with his men and fought valiantly until the fighting was over. The firing was sharp and deadly on both sides as the remaining eight companies of the regiment hustled into line, taking cover behind the large boulders about a quarter of the way down the hill and began to blaze away.[121]

At one point, Pvt. Samuel Hazen of Co. G acted as a medic. He set to work binding up the wrist of a wounded man in the 16th Michigan, for whom the arrival of the 140th New York was no less miraculous than if it had been a legion of angels from heaven.[122]

The suddenness of the attack caught many Confederates in no-man's land. "Such of the Rebels as had approached so near as to make escape almost impossible dropped their guns, threw up their hands, and upon a slight slackening of our fire rushed in upon us and gave themselves as prisoners, while those not so near took advantage of the chance left them and retreated in disorder," remembered Lt. Farley.[123]

The completed line of the 140th New York formed an inverted "V," part of it facing south toward Big Round Top and the rest facing west toward Devil's Den in the valley below. The main Confederate attack was blunted, but for some time there was still a large amount of lead in the air. As soon as practical, some soldiers carried the body of Col. O'Rorke the few rods behind Little Round Top, where the regimental surgeons, Dr. Dean and Dr. Lord had set up an aid station. But it was hopeless. A bloody froth on each side of the young colonel's neck showed the fatal track of the wound. The colonel was dead. Bought with his life though, was another saving moment for the Union on Little Round Top.[124]

As another lull came, Lt. Hazlett's first two guns fired from the summit and the 140th New York was ordered to reform closer to the top of the hill, to more closely support Hazlett's Battery there. The men had a quick time of it, trying to get back while still under fire. "We were placed in front of their guns only leaving narrow spaces for them to fire through. The concussion injured the hearing of quite a number of our regiment," remembered Pvt. Hazen. "After the battery fired a while, we were ordered to the southwest slope of Little Round Top again." Such was the confusion on the hill at that time. Perhaps the staff officer that caused that movement was the same that had supposedly been calling Welch's men earlier — to scoot back up to the summit of Little Round Top, to protect those guns. The exact truth may never be known.[125]

Rochester Historical Society

Dr. Mathias L. Lord, Surgeon, 140th New York.

MOLLUS

Lt. Charles E. Hazlett, Co. D, 5th U.S. Artillery.

Property of
Lodi Memorial Library

Photo by Author

Hazlett's guns on Little Round Top today.

Reinforcements began to arrive, the rest of Gen. Stephen Weed's Brigade which had initially gone on to support Sickles' Third Corps, but were then ordered to turn about and double-quick back up to Little Round Top instead. And a welcome sight they must have been; those men of the 91st Pennsylvania, 146th New York and 155th Pennsylvania. The rest of Hazlett's artillery guns opened, six guns in all, pouring death and destruction down the hill and into the valley below.[126]

Captain Frank C. Gibbs' Battery L, 1st Ohio Light Artillery was not far behind, taking a position to Hazlett's right on the northern slope of Little Round Top. The ground there was so rough that the guns had to be muscled in by hand. But, the deed was done and Gibbs immediately started working his guns as well.[127]

When Col. Vincent was mortally wounded, command devolved onto the shoulders of Col. James C. Rice, 44th New York, sometimes called "Old Crazy" by his men for his excitable manner, especially under fire. But on this day, Col. Rice was cool and resolute while conducting military operations. Rice could be seen encouraging his men, steadying his lines, while making necessary adjustments to

Col. James C. Rice, 44th New York.
MOLLUS

strengthen his position. The 34-year-old Yale grad and lawyer from New York City was well prepared for his role in the action on Little Round Top. He would not let Vincent or his country down.[128]

Stand Firm 'Ye Boys From Maine!

Again the Rebels were preparing for another assault, this time on the Union left again. On they came in a crash. Chamberlain later recalled:

> The two lines met and broke and mingled in the shock. The crush of musketry gave way to cuts and thrusts, grappling and wrestlings. The edge of the conflict swayed to and fro, with wild whirlpools and eddies. At times I saw around me more of the enemy than of my own men; gaps opening, swallowing, closing again with sharp convulsive energy; squads of stalwart men who had cut their way through us, disappearing as if translated. All around strange mingled roar....[129]

> In the very deepest of the struggle while our shattered line had pressed the enemy well below their first point of contact and the struggle to regain it was fierce, I saw a sudden rift in the thick smoke our colors standing alone... In the center, wreathed in battle smoke stood Color Sgt. Andrew J. Tozier. His color-staff planted in the ground at his side, the upper part clasped in his elbow, so holding the flag upright with musket and cartridges seized from the fallen comrade at his side he was defending his sacred trust in the manner of the songs of chivalry.[130]

Through the smoke, Chamberlain had seen Tozier firing a rifle he had picked up from a wounded soldier. From the far left wing Capt. Spear also recalled seeing Sgt. Tozier, clinging fast to the Colors, loading and firing in the thickening haze, and while discharging his duties, was "chewing on a piece of cartridge paper," torn from a bullet. The moment was locked in memory's glance forever.[131]

But other members of the Color Guard were there too: Pvt. Elisha Coan, Cpl. William T. Livermore, Cpl. Charlie Reed, wounded in the wrist, and Cpl. Melville C. Day, lying there with 5 shots in his body, dying. "Stand firm ye boys from Maine," wrote Pvt. Theodore Gerrish years after the war, describing those scenes and capturing the thoughts and feelings of their colonel and each man on the line. (See interesting note on Pvt. Gerrish).[132]

And stood they did as the hailstorm of lead was poured upon them. Chamberlain limped along the line after being struck twice; once in the right instep by a piece of shell or splintered rock, tearing his boot, blood oozing, and again by another ball that came crashing from the left but struck his steel scabbard and was deflected, leaving only a painful contusion on his left thigh as a reminder of his good fortune. But there was no time to attend to his own needs. More pressing matters lay to his front. With the center about to go down, Col. Chamberlain sent his brother, Lt. Thomas Chamberlain, to help save the colors. He also sent Sgt. Ruel Thomas in case his brother should fail. The Confederate advance pressed Chamberlain's left almost back upon his right and the 20th Maine line took on the shape of a hairpin as the life and death grapple continued.[133]

During one of these thrusts, Col. Oates' young brother, Lt. John A. Oates, who had been sick but refused his brother's urgings not to go into the fight, was mortally wounded when struck by several balls. When John went down on the field, Lt. Isaac H. Parks, an old schoolmate, ran over to help him and dragged him behind a large boulder nearby. And even as Parks let him down behind the rock, another bullet struck John in one of his hands, taking away his little finger. There was not much more that his old school friend could have done for him. Oates later recalled that when he advised his brother to sit the battle out, his brother doggedly replied, "Brother, I will not do it. If I were to remain here people would say that I did it through cowardice; no, sir, I am an officer and will never disgrace the uniform I wear; I shall go through, unless I am killed, which I think is quite likely." Young Oates' fears became reality. He was captured and lived but 23 days. His brother never saw him alive again. The struggle on Little Round Top continued until once again the Maine men beat back their foe.[134]

Another lull came. As Chamberlain moved along his line to check on his men, he came upon the wrecked body of Pvt. George Washington Buck of Co. H, in the area of his bent back left wing, lying with a mortal wound in his right shoulder. Buck had been a sergeant at the Battle of Fredericksburg, but was the victim of a bullying quartermaster who took his stripes away for refusing to perform a menial task. It was an injustice the proud soldier did not seek to rectify, but Chamberlain had kept it in mind for early action. Now lying there, life ebbing away, the colonel restored his honor. Buck whispered, "Tell my mother I did not die a coward!" It was the prayer of home-bred manhood poured out with his life-blood. "I knew and answered him," recalled Chamberlain. "You die a sergeant! I promote you for faithful service and noble courage on the field of Gettysburg!" This was all he wanted, nothing more.[135]

Chamberlain moved on to attend to the other wounded and the other needs of his men. "Ammunition!" was the cry heard along the line. Their supply was dangerously low, in fact almost gone. With sixty rounds to a man they had filled the air and a number of Confederate bodies with over twenty thousand bullets. The men could not withstand another assault. And as the firing on the other side of Little Round Top was still raging out of his view, Chamberlain wondered if the hill was being surrounded. Half his command was down. Chamberlain remembered, "My thought was running deep." Hurriedly, he called a conference to deal with the matter.[136]

In the meantime, Capt. D. B. Waddell, adjutant of the 15th Alabama, had gotten approval from Col. Oates to take 40 or 50 men from the right wing of the regiment and assault the 20th Maine from the furthest point of the Confederate right, to try to turn the taunt and stretched Union line once and for all. Waddell and his men moved out.[137]

Weed Comes Up On The Right

Brigadier Gen. Stephen H. Weed was a West Pointer, graduating in 1854 a bit above the middle of his class. And as the rest of his brigade filed into position of support to the right of the 140th New York, he surveyed the field with Gen. Warren and Gen. Sykes as Lt. Charles Hazlett sat on his horse at the summit of Little Round Top directing the artillery operations of his battery. At the beginning of the day's events, Lt. Hazlett had confided to his commander Capt. Augustus P. Martin, Chief of Artillery for the Fifth Corps, that he was feeling uncomfortable, saying, "I have just received bad news from home and I would rather someone else would lead to-day, besides," he said, "I have (had) a premonition that this will be my last battle." It was rather odd, for Capt. Martin had never known Hazlett to hesitate. But Martin calmed his young artillery lieutenant by telling Hazlett that he had the utmost confidence in him and the cloud of doubt disappeared.

MOLLUS

Brig. Gen. Stephen H. Weed.

Captain Martin had a special regard for Hazlett's capabilities and wanted him at his right hand. General Warren did not know if artillery could be particularly useful on Little Round Top, but Lt. Hazlett told him, "Never mind that. The sound of my guns will be encouraging for our troops and disheartening to the others, and my battery's of no use if this hill is lost!" And though Hazlett's guns did not have much impact against Confederates on Little Round Top, they certainly played havoc with enemy troops in the Valley of Death below.[138]

As the Union "hail" of mini balls and cannon balls rained down on the Confederates below Little Round Top, Rebel sharpshooters busied themselves attempting to pick off the Federal gunners. While talking with Lt. Hazlett, Gen. Warren was grazed in the throat by a bullet, but luckily the wound was not serious.[139] Not long afterward, however, a sniper's bullet found its mark when a ball stuck Gen. Weed, passing through his spine, paralyzing the lower part of his body. The wound was mortal. Weed called out for his friend Lt. Hazlett who kneeled down to hear the general's dying words. At that moment, another bullet crashed into the back of Hazlett's skull. He slumped over his leader and never spoke again, dying about 8:00 p.m. Command of the guns devolved upon the shoulders of Lt. Benjamin F. Rittenhouse, who worked them with a vengeance.

General Weed was carried off the field to the aid station behind Little Round Top where surgeons might attend to him. His aide, Lt. William H. Crennell, tried to comfort him saying, "General, I hope that you are not so badly hurt." To this Weed replied, "I'm as dead a man as Julius Ceasar." Weed would linger for a while but his fate was inevitable. Crennell noted afterward in his diary that it was about 9:05 p.m. when the General breathed his last.[140]

The Confederate assault subsided on the right. But the Union artillery kept blazing away, pouring a hot fire down the slopes and into the valley, trying to tilt the scales of victory in their favor as one last desperate attempt by the Confederates under Oates against the Union left was about to get under way.

"Bayonet... Forward!" Approx. 6:45 p.m.

Advance or retreat? "It must not be the latter, but how can it be the former?" Chamberlain understood how it could be done.[141] Lieutenant Holman S. Melcher of the 20th Maine's Co. F advanced a plea to his colonel to go forward and cover the wounded who lay in agony. Chamberlain said, "Yes sir, in a moment! I am about to order a charge!" The colonel then told Capt. Ellis Spear, Co. G commander on his far bent back left to thrust forward while the 20th Maine center held fast on the colors. And as the left swung down and to the right and met the center line, the rest of the regiment would join the

Pejepscot Historical Society

Col. Joshua L. Chamberlain, 20th Maine.

Maine State Archives

Capt. Ellis Spear, 20th Maine.

sweeping movement. It was a textbook maneuver. The men took their places as Chamberlain hobbled over to Capt. A. W. Clark on the right of his line, to tell him to hold fast to the left of the 83rd Pennsylvania when the charge was made. As the Rebel lines had again formed and were seen advancing, Chamberlain stepped to the colors with his sword extended and a single word reverberated along his line. "BAYONET!"[142]

The metallic clash of steel made the line quiver. And in the welling of hearts, minds and souls, the men rose as one. Before Chamberlain could finish the verbal command, Lt. Holman Melcher leapt forward with the battle cry, "Come on! Come on! Come on boys!" matching Chamberlain's guttural groan, "Forward — to the right!" The men took up the roar. Captain Ellis Spear and his men of Co. G. at the far left flung themselves down the slope as the screams and profanities married the sounds of musketry and mayhem that accompany such actions of men.[143]

Down the hill they swept, like a swinging gate those boys from Maine, firing if they had a shot left or raising hell in battle cry otherwise, while jumping over the dead and in between the wounded men, zig-zagging their way through the trees, thrusting, slashing, always pressing the enemy. The surprise was such that the first line of Confederates dropped their weapons and gave up, dazed by their charging foe. In a moment of shock, catching the "Rebs" leaning backward, the Union onslaught gained the decided advantage.[144]

MOLLUS

Lt. Holman S. Melcher, 20th Maine.

Colonel William C. Oates of the 15th Alabama tried to rally his men but it was hopeless. The Union men came on in a rush, crashing, in hand to hand grapplings. In the close contact of combatants, a Maine man reached for the colors of the 15th Alabama, some two or three steps to the right of a large boulder, on the extreme Union left. The color bearer, Ensign Archibald, stepped

Photo by Author

The "famous" Oates rock is easy to locate today on that bent back portion of the 20th Maine's Union line. Oates claimed Capt. Waddell's force reached this point just before being turned back by the charging Maine men. Years later, Col. Oates wanted to place a small monument near this rock, as witness to the fact. But it was not to be. (See "Little Round Top Talk" for more).

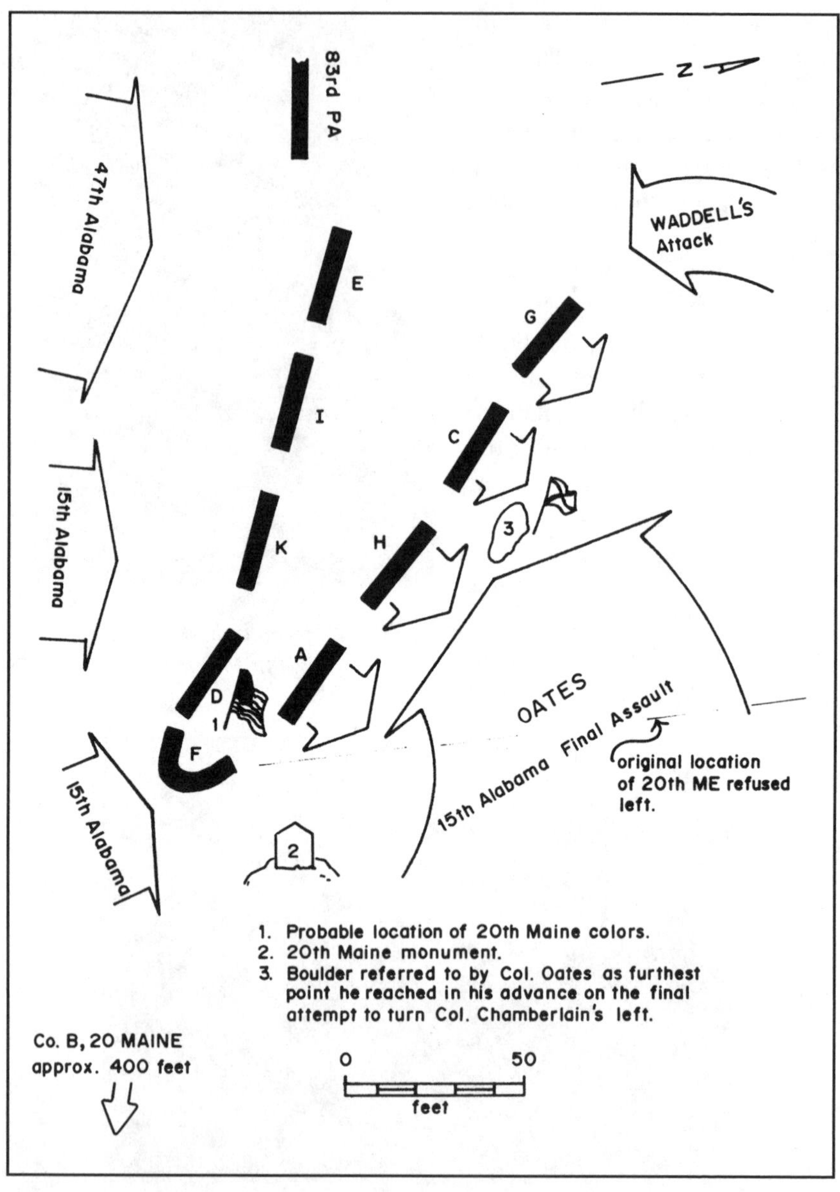

Approx. 6:45 p.m. — Chamberlain's battle line, and how it was pressed back by the repeated onslaught of the 47th and 15th Alabama regiments. With his men almost out of ammunition, Chamberlain makes the critical decision. In one word he ignites his men. "Bayonet!" They rise along the bent back line, and become "like a swinging gate," charging down the slope and sweeping the field of Confederates.

back and Sgt. Pat O'Connor forced his bayonet into the head of the Maine soldier. But the thrust of the charging Maine men was overwhelming and the Confederate position no longer tenable.

The roar of the Maine men was deafening, while the fighting spirit of the Alabamians was fading. Captain Waddell, in his attempt at an heroic act, was caught in a bad spot but somehow got away from the charging Yankees, avoiding capture. But many of his men were nabbed.

Just when it seemed that things could get no worse for the Rebels they did. For now, from the far left, behind a stone wall, rose the all-but-forgotten Capt. Walter G. Morrill and his 50 men from Co. B, and probably some of the 10 or 15 Stoughton's Sharpshooters who had been driven over Big Round Top by Col. Oates earlier in the battle. And perhaps a few of the men from the "lost 16th Michigan skirmishers," got into the mix.[145]

The crashing volley poured into the rear of the faltering Confederate ranks of the 15th and 47th Alabama regiments. Captain Morrill and his men then made loud demonstrations, with shouts of "Charge!" and the like, to make the Alabamians think that they were being attacked by a much larger force.

The shock threw the Rebels into a state of panic. Morrill's men confronted some fleeing Confederates by a "worm fence lane" north of their position and also exchanged shots with some of Capt. Shaaf's Alabamians, near the northeast base of Big Round Top. A brief stand was made part way up Big Round Top by Shaaf and his men who had been joined by the exiting Capt. Waddell and the remnant of his group in an all-out effort to avoid capture. Morrill's sharpshooters chased them, but soon stopped and returned to their original position be-

Maine State Archives

Capt. Walter G. Morrill, 20th Maine.

hind the stone wall, so as not to risk getting out of position and being unable to provide support for the regiment.

Morrill knew his orders. The best that the Rebels could do in that part of the field was to chew up some timber, while filling the air with lead in the hope of stalling the Union advance. But everywhere else Confederates were running, tripping, falling, trying to get away. As the sweeping 20th Maine line continued the pivoting movement, they were joined by the skirmishers of the 83rd Pennsylvania on their right. It became a rout.[146]

To Chamberlain's front, a Confederate officer later identified as Lt. Robert Wicker fired his pistol almost in Chamberlain's face, but missed, and then surrendered when the colonel piqued his throat with his sword and relieved the officer of his fine Navy Colt revolver, which was put into immediate use to aid the Union cause.[147]

Oates observed that his men were getting hit from all angles. "While one man was shot in the face, his right hand or left hand comrade was shot in the side or back. Some were struck simultaneously with two or three balls from different directions." Oates said later that he then ordered a retreat, but it is unlikely that any such order was truly transmitted through the ranks, for his Confederate forces were already in full retreat. "When the signal was given," Oates claimed, "we ran like a herd of wild cattle, right through the line of dismounted cavalrymen." Clearly, Oates was confused, for there was no report of Union cavalry operating in the vicinity.[148]

As Oates took flight with his boys, a man named John Keels of Co. H, who was running behind him and on his right was shot in the throat, blood spattering all over. Oates watched him run across the mountain, his windpipe severed, breathing out his neck. Keels' wound was mortal and he died soon thereafter. Oates almost got captured himself when he began to faint from exhaustion during the retreat over Big Round Top, but was revived when a regimental surgeon, Dr. Reeves, poured water on his head. He then turned command over to Capt. Blant A. Hill temporarily, with orders to reform the regiments in the open field at the western base of Big Round Top. The order was obeyed.[149]

Left behind the fleeing Confederates were their dead and wounded, lying in groups or huddled alone behind cover such as they could find. One Union soldier came upon the wrecked body of Lt.

Col. Michael J. Bulger, lying against a tree and losing blood fast. The Union soldier swiped the colonel's hat off his head and placed it upon his own head and mockingly ordered Bulger to hand up his sword and pistol.

Bulger refused to surrender his sword to the soldier saying, "My good fellow, is it possible that you are a federal soldier, and in the army of the United States, and yet you do not know that a private is not authorized to disarm an officer he captures?" The Union private, seeing that the colonel was in no shape to escape, gleefully ran off to get just such a man. Soon, a Union colonel, probably Chamberlain, came up to Bulger and took the official surrender. Bulger was a proud man, though probably should not have been on the field or in the army at his age. Chamberlain did what he could to comfort Bulger until he could be removed for proper medical care. He survived his wound and was kept prisoner at Johnson's Island, near Sandusky, Ohio, until exchanged in April 1864.[150]

Further along the line, Col. Chamberlain and Capt. O.S. Woodward met another Confederate officer, Col. Robert M. Powell of the 5th Texas, whose men had been hammering away at the lines of the 44th New York and the 16th Michigan. Powell was severely wounded, his gaping chest wound oozing blood and life with it. He had seen his command literally disintegrate right before his eyes.

It was ironic how, as the battle faded, Col. Powell lifted his head up and looked back at the retreating Confederate line to notice Sgt. Ross from his regiment, while simply walking down the slope, stop and leisurely pick up a ramrod that was leaning against a rock, then continue into the cover of the woods. All Powell could do was wait for help from the Union soldiers that moved forward as the Confederates vacated the field.[151]

It was in this moment of frustration that Col. Powell stated to Capt. Woodward, with Col. Chamberlain probably within earshot, "You have peppered us pretty badly, but you'll get the worst of it before it's over!" He was led away to the field hospital of the 83rd Pennsylvania for treatment. He would survive the battle and the war, being held prisoner until exchanged on Feb. 2, 1865.[152]

Such a spirited momentum did Col. Chamberlain's men exhibit as they swept the field that he later wrote, "they thought they were on the road to Richmond!" He halted his cheering line near the front of the 44th New York and reformed his men at their original position on the line, but not before gathering about 400 prisoners. And as the sounds of musketry faded off, the field became quiet except for the groans of the wounded and dying, lying among the rocks and slumped near trees, waiting for help to come. Quickly, they tended to those in need, both North and South.[153]

The 44th New York took their share of prisoners. When the fighting ended, 1st Sergeant Consider A. Willet of Co. E saw numerous Confederates stranded on the slope to his front. Taking a half dozen men along, he went out to bring them in. The 44th counted 90 prisoners to their credit. One prisoner begged Capt. Nathaniel Husted not to be shot. As he did so, he was struck in the back by a Confederate ball probably meant for Capt. Husted. Such is the factor of chance on the battlefield.[154]

Another unlucky Rebel was John W. Stevens of the 5th Texas. While taking cover behind the shelter of a rock, he was sure his Texas compatriots would soon be returning for yet another go at the Union line, but was surprised when a sword blade slapped him across the back, and an order came for him to throw down his gun. Caught in a fix, he complied and lived to tell about it. But first he would have to settle for some Union hospitality in a prison camp.[155]

Maine State Archives

Sgt. Albert E. Fernald, 20th Maine.

Among the wounded of the 20th Maine was a young 24-year-old tailor named Sgt. Albert E. Fernald of Co. K, shot in the hip. A noted historian dubbed him "a human bombshell" and it probably was a bad idea for the Confederates to have hit him at Gettysburg. For Fernald came back to fight even more fiercely on other fields, charging and capturing an artillery piece in the Battle of Peebles Farm, Va., and charging the enemy works again at the Battle of Five Forks, near the end of the War, coming out of that fight with the flag of the

9th Virginia Infantry and a Medal of Honor to boot. Five feet, five inches of sheer terror, Fernald proved that heroes come in all sizes.

As the smoke settled on Little Round Top, the sun dipped below the horizon and shadows began to fall. Another sunset was upon them. But for some lying there in death's fixed gaze, there would be no more. Already crimson pools were gathering at body's lowest point and puddles of blood formed on the rocks, on the ledges and even began to seep into the Pennsylvania soil below.[156]

Big Round Top

Colonel Rice, having done a superb job since taking command after Col. Vincent fell, scanned his front and focused his attention on a new concern, Big Round Top. What could the Confederates do, if they could hold it? The sun had set and it was growing dark, especially under the trees with their summer foliage, when more reinforcements began to arrive.

It was Col. Joseph W. Fisher's Brigade of the 3rd Division. Rice asked Fisher to move forward and occupy Big Round Top with his Pennsylvania Reserves, but Fisher balked. Chamberlain later recalled that Fisher, "emphatically declined; and I remember his saying that his men were armed with some inefficient rifle — 'smooth bores' it seems to me he said — & especially that the ground was difficult & unknown to his men. He & his men also were much agitated."[157]

In view of the circumstances, Col. Fisher probably wanted his superior, Gen. Samuel W. Crawford, to approve before committing his troops to such a dangerous mission. And so the conference went. Initially, Fisher did decline Col. Rice's request to take and secure Big Round Top, but he sent a messenger to Gen. Crawford. It was not what Col. Rice wanted to hear. That hill must be secured and there was little time to bicker with "who" should do the taking.

Colonel Rice then turned to Chamberlain and his tired, worn, and weary Maine men and made his request. Night had fallen, and the men had already started to settle down to catch some sleep. "They were lying on their arms — all but a few pickets — in a sleep like a swoon," Chamberlain later wrote. "I had not the heart to order the poor fellows up," he remembered. But necessity dictated otherwise. "Boys, I am asked if I can carry that hill in front!" was the summons. His men answered in a resounding cheer. "Yes!" And so it was ordered.[158]

So, as fresh men stood fast, men almost spent from fighting gathered up their equipment as Chamberlain later recalled, "Without waiting to get ammunition, but trusting in part to the very circumstances of not exposing our movement or our small front by firing, and with bayonets fixed, the little handful of 200 men [including Capt. Morrill's Company B] pressed up the moutainside in very extended order, as the steep and jagged surface of the ground compelled." It was about 9:00 p.m., with a bright moon rising in the east.[159]

Chamberlain's men moved out. Step by step, they made their way among the rocks and boulders to the summit of Big Round Top. As they pushed forward there was scattered fire coming from Confederate guns, aiming at noises in the darkness. But the Rebels were firing over the heads of Chamberlain's men, a common problem in night firing, when marksmen tend to shoot high. At this point some Confederates were captured by the Maine men, including Lt. Thomas Christian of General Law's staff.[160]

Arriving at the crest, Chamberlain drew his troops together, forming a solid front. Shortly after coming to a halt and into position, a picket line was sent out to guard against any surprise Confederate attack. Within about a half hour, there was more noise of movement on Chamberlain's right. It was Col. Fisher's 9th and 10th Pennsylvania Reserves.

Apparently Col. Fisher finally got permission from Gen. Crawford to move out after Crawford had made his way to Little Round Top sometime later, to see what was going on. Crawford later acknowledged a type of meeting with Col. Rice in his battlefield report. But as the two regiments started groping up the hillside, moving "by the right flank," and having difficulty getting into line and into place, Chamberlain and his Maine men thought that they might be Confederates poking around their flank, trying to separate them from the brigade. So they made "dispositions to receive them as such. In the confusion which attended the attempt to form them in support of my right, the enemy opened a brisk fire, which disconcerted my efforts to form them and disheartened the supports themselves," Chamberlain later wrote in his battle report. It was enough to send Fisher's men into a spin and they quickly retreated back down Big Round Top to safety. They would not be back anytime soon.[161]

It was a dangerous situation. Chamberlain quickly divided his regiment, half holding their places on the summit of Big Round Top and the other half withdrawing to the ground abandoned by the support troops half way down the hill on his right rear. He could not afford to get cut off and isolated from the rest of the brigade. He immediately sent for the 83rd Pennsylvania to come to his aid.

The 83rd showed up soon afterward, with fresh ammo and the 44th New York, to add a little more muscle to the right of the 20th Maine line. The ammunition was quickly distributed. Chamberlain then formed two reliefs of skirmishers, or pickets, that changed every two hours, allowing the men to "sleep on their arms," while others watched. As diligent as he was brave, he posted the picket and ordered the officers in charge to report conditions to him every half hour."[162]

It was not long before the men on picket duty, filing down the western slope of Big Round Top until they could catch a glimpse of the enemy by the light of their campfires, encountered some movement to their front. "Who goes there?" one Maine man ordered. "We're 4th Texas," was the reply. "All right, come on," one of the Mainers answered, "We're 4th Texas." And as the Southerners moved forward they heard the sound of weapons being cocked. One by one, and in groups, they were duped and bagged. This strategy was continued until twenty-five of the 4th Texas had been captured by the Maine men of Co. E on the right of the line.[163]

Later that night, about midnight, Col. Fisher came up again with two of his regiments. This time they took a position on the left of the 20th Maine. As the enemy did not threaten in that area, Col. Chamberlain made no attempt to connect with them. But any additional support was welcomed. The advanced position on Big Round Top was secure.

In the early morning, however, there was some sharp skirmishing in front of the 20th Maine position and Lt. Arad Linscott of Co. I took a musket and went out in advance of the picket line to get a shot at the enemy, but got himself shot instead. A Rebel sharpshooter wounded him in the thigh, the wound being mortal. Linscott, an officer who showed much promise and was a favorite of Col. Chamberlain's, died some three weeks later, on July 27, after being furloughed home. Another fine officer was lost in the Union cause.[164]

There was more sharp skirmishing at daylight, and perhaps many of the men thought that was a sure sign of action coming their way again. A strong Confederate skirmish line was seen to their right front, but it came to a halt and advanced no further. Soon afterward the firing subsided. The battle for the Round Tops was over.[165]

Woe! The Cost of War!

Along the line of the brigade, the wounded were brought in and cared for by the heavily taxed medical corps as every house and barn was converted into a hospital, an operating room and in many places adjacent, a mortuary or burial ground. Everywhere lay the dead, some with contorted faces, in shocked anger of departure from life so young, robbed of a future filled with hopes and dreams. And still others looking almost angelic; facial forms serene. Men vomited as on battlefields before and since at the battle carnage before them.

Lieutenant Porter Farley, adjutant of the 140th New York, was overcome with grief at the loss of his commander, Col. O'Rorke:

> Up to that time in my life I had never felt a grief so sharply, nor realized the significance of death so well as then... To me and all of us he had seemed so near the beau ideal of a soldier and a gentleman, all that he had been and the bright promise of what he was to be was so fresh in our minds, and now, in an instant, the fatal bullet had cut short the chapter of that fair life... For him to die was to me like losing a brother, and that brother almost the perfection of the manly graces... I took from his pockets his watch and some trifles, pulled from his hands the long gloves which he had worn and slipped them in his belt, helped compose his supple form in a fitting way, collected the men who had brought him and others to the surgeon's station, and taking a long look at poor O'Rorke went back to the regiment.[166]

The bodies of Gen. Weed, Col. O'Rorke, and Lt. Charles Hazlett had been carried to the Weikert farm house and placed side by side covered with sheets. Hazlett's body was buried in Weikert's garden, but the bodies of Weed and O'Rorke were moved back to another hospital area on the Lewis A. Bushman farm. They were buried "in (the) rear of his house on the west side of the first apple tree," wrote Lt. Crennell (Weed's aide), in his diary.[167]

Among the fallen, just to the front of the 140th New York's Co. C position, was young Pvt. John Allen, only sixteen years old. Having concealed his youth upon enlistment, he was found out and was to be sent home. Somehow, he managed to stay with the regiment to see this one battle. He was granted his wish but it cost him his life. He was buried there on the hill. His loss so grieved his mother that she had his letters read to her every night for the remainder of her life.

Allen's body was among those later reinterred in the National Cemetery at Gettysburg. Also, just to the front of the 140th New York line, was the lifeless body of a Confederate soldier literally riddled with bullets, seventeen in all. Such was the traffic of death missiles on the hill that day.[168]

Courtesy Richard Leisenring Collection

Pvt. John Allen (age 16), 140th New York.

Soldiers combing the front of the 83rd Pennsylvania's position found Pvt. Philip Grine of Co. H, his body now still. During a lull in the fighting this brave Union soldier ventured forward to bring in a wounded Confederate. The wounded Rebel soldier was laid on a stretcher and carried off to the hospital. Private Grine went out a second time and brought in another. Fatigued from his exertions, he asked some of his comrades to go along and assist him in bringing in others. They went out with him, saw the Rebels posted behind the rocks firing at them, and refused to go any further. Grine went alone and never came back.[169]

Burial details were busy into the night. The men did their best to get something to eat and steal some sleep, for they knew the next day would be more of the same. They had learned to be survivors. Camp fires scribed the new lines in the dark of night as a bright moon arched across the sky, a night sentinel, as both armies rested.

The Morning's Light, July 3rd

The morning coffee was welcomed as the troops on Little Round Top and Big Round Top tried to shake awake and clear their heads for another day of battle. From which direction did not matter, for the left was reinforced now. Colonel Rice made his way along the line, full of congratulatory remarks for the men. He approached Col. Chamberlain and said warmly, "Your gallantry was magnificent and your coolness saved us." Rice, though an intensely emotional officer, was in Chamberlain's opinion, "as brave and true a man as ever went 'booted and spurred' from the field." He was also generous, complimenting Chamberlain in his official report, not only for his actions on Little Round Top, but Big Round Top as well.[170]

Other field and staff officers were also busy moving among their troops, congratulating them on a job well done, while making last minute adjustments to further strengthen their positions. And though many a brave comrade had fallen, including the gallant Vincent, O'Rorke, Weed and Hazlett, the men of the brigade knew they had accomplished something unique in the defense of the Round Tops.

At about 9:00 a.m., word came that the brigade would be relieved by the fresh troops of Col. Fisher's Brigade. The brigade would go into a reserve position behind the left-center of Meade's main line on Cemetery Ridge. This placed them to the left of the point of Lee's great assault which would become known as "Pickett's Charge." Though Rice's Brigade did not participate directly in the defense of the line on the third day of fighting, it was under heavy artillery fire that afternoon.[171]

A Last Moment of Tension

As the regiments formed their lines to march off Little Round Top, Lt. Col. Norval E. Welch returned with his 45 men of the 16th Michigan, "absentees" from the last moments of critical fighting in the battle the day before. A moment of tension resulted. What could Col. Vincent's bugler, Pvt. Oliver W. Norton have been thinking when these men returned? Norton had gone, immediately after battle, to see about Vincent. He found Lt. Col. Welch and several of his "flying men" clearly more than a mile and half away from the battle at the Bushman farm-house-turned hospital site, where Vincent lay dying. There Welch had told Vincent that the regiment had been driven from the field.[172] How could he say that to Norton, who was firing a musket only minutes before right next to the men who had remained on the hill where Vincent had fallen while trying to check that retreat. Norton likely recalled his commander lying on his deathbed, his face lit with a smile when Norton said, "The boys are still there Colonel!" Nostrils must have been flaring.[173]

Colonel Rice too, probably saw red when Welch and his men reappeared. Initially, Rice would not allow the colors back into the 16th Michigan line. This caused a stir. Major Robert Elliott, Capt. Benjamin F. Partridge, and others of the 16th Michigan, all who had fought valiantly during the defense of Little Round Top, refused to march off the hill without their colors. Faced with mutiny and possibly an embarrassing investigation, Col. Rice relented and had Welch and the others returned to the ranks.[174]

Onto the Blazoned Pages of History!

Lines straightened and tempers calmed, Col. Rice's brigade marched off Little Round Top and onto the blazoned pages of history. The South never came so close to victory at Gettysburg as they did at Little Round Top on the second day of the battle. Had they succeeded there, they surely would have caused a major disruption in Meade's line of defense and perhaps have caused Meade to recoil — change his front — or even "flinch" and retreat.

Meade was a good commander, but he had only been in command of the Army of the Potomac a scant five days. Though he knew Lincoln wanted him to be aggressive in giving battle to Lee's Army, he also knew it should not be at the expense of exposing Baltimore or Washington to attack, which could have had catastrophic consequences. And, in the back of his mind, he still had the original "Pipe Creek" Plan, a defensive plan to protect both Baltimore and Washington while giving battle to the enemy. He had to be very wary of Lee, who had demonstrated his mastery of military tactics on fields before, dominating his Union counterparts with less men and material.

While some historians say that Meade still had the entire Sixth Corps in reserve, available to aid the Union left if that flank was turned and the line started to crumble, it is not certain that he would have taken that great a gamble at Gettysburg. Meade was a professional soldier and his entire war record shows him to have been a good fighter. But he was not a great risk taker, such as Grant or Sheridan. No one knows how Meade would have reacted if the tide of battle had turned. But one thing is certain. If Lee had succeeded in turning the Union left on July 2 at Little Round Top, there would have been no need for Pickett's Charge on the third day. Clearly, Lee had a better opportunity at Little Round Top to achieve his goal.[175]

Property of
Lodi Memorial Library

The Aftermath

Col. Strong Vincent

Shortly after being wounded in the left side groin area, Col. Vincent was carried off to the Lewis A. Bushman farm house, about one and a half miles from Little Round Top, where surgeons determined that his wound was fatal. Unable to be moved, Vincent requested that they send for his wife, Elizabeth. Lieutenant John M. Clark mounted his horse and rode forty miles to Westminster, Maryland, to telegraph her. Another officer dashed off to Hanover to send another telegram should the first one fail. It was a wish that regrettably would go unfulfilled. Elizabeth, far into her pregnancy, was in no condition to travel, but her father-in-law left Erie immediately after receiving notice of his son's wounding.

Vincent was visited on July 3 by Gen. Daniel Butterfield, who expressed his deep concern over Vincent's wounding but was congratulatory in expressing the nation's gratitude for what he and his brigade had done to save the day at Little Round Top. Butterfield also told him that he had already, by direction of Gen. Meade, telegraphed for his appointment as a brigadier general.[176]

For the next few days, the parade of generals included Gen. Sykes and Gen. Barnes, Vincent's immediate commander, and other prominent officers who had come to know and respect him. "I presume," said Vincent, "I have done my last fighting," trying to make light of a grim situation. But after two days his desire to speak lessened, his life ebbing away. Dr. Burchfield, the regimental surgeon of the 83rd Pennsylvania, did all he could, but it did not save him. His wound was inoperable. Lieutenant Clark, assistant adjutant to Vincent, was always nearby to comfort his commander.[177]

Vincent lingered for five days, while a well deserved promotion to brigadier general was hurriedly applied for by General Meade:

> Maj. Gen. H.W. Hallack July 3, 1863
>
> I would respectfully request that Col. Strong Vincent, Eighty-third Pennsylvania Regiment, be made a brigadier general of volunteers for gallant conduct on the field yesterday. He is mortally

wounded, and it would gratify his friends, as well as myself. It was my intention to have recommended him with others, should he live. Among the general officers wounded to-day I omitted to mention in previous dispatch Major-General Butterfield, not seriously, and Major-General Doubleday.

Geo. G. Meade
Major-General[178]

The next morning at 10:05 a.m., the reply came from none other than the Secretary of War, Edwin M. Stanton:

Major General MEADE, Headquarters:

War Department
Washington, D.C. July 4, 1863

According to your request, Colonel Vincent has been appointed brigadier general for gallant service on the field. This department will rejoice to manifest honor and gratitude to you and your gallant comrades in arms.

Edwin M. Stanton
Secretary of War[179]

Secretary Stanton, long an opponent of deathbed promotions, who often needed prodding by the president to act upon them, probably saw Vincent's promotion as extraordinary indeed and acted quickly upon its approval.[180]

Historians have doubted whether such order or approval reached Vincent before he died. This is probably due to the nebulous character of the flow of communications in and around Gettysburg during the period, and the absence of clear documentation of the arrival of such orders by Union officers on the scene who could have witnessed an actual notification to Vincent. As the telegraph lines were down around the battle area and communications were received either from Westminster, Hanover, or perhaps Taneytown, it is difficult to pinpoint at exactly what time a communiqué may have arrived at Meade's headquarters. But in this matter specifically, considering the fact that Gen. Meade took such pains to make the recommendation in the midst of the still-critical battle situation, one might also assume its reply was just as important. And when the telegram of approval was received, it would have surely been speedily delivered to Vincent's bedside.

Colonel Strong Vincent's sufferings, though they must have been excruciating, were borne without complaint, and his last conscious words were the repetition of the Lord's Prayer; evidence of his strong

Episcopal faith. He died on July 7, 1863, before his father could reach him.[181]

The next day, Lt. John M. Clark proceeded to Erie with Vincent's remains. Vincent's father arrived on the battlefield on July 8, after several days' delay, too late to find his son there. The next best thing the senior Vincent could do was to inquire about and locate the remains of another son of Erie who fell; Capt. John M. Sell also of the 83rd Pennsylvania. Vincent made the necessary arrangements and quickly left on his return to Erie to attend his beloved son's funeral.

Elizabeth, then seven months into her pregnancy, attended the funeral, held on Monday, July 13, in the Vincent home. The procession moved from the residence of Vincent's father to St. Paul's Church in Erie for an impressive memorial service. He was buried with full military honors.[182]

On September 29, 1863, a daughter, Blanche Strong Vincent was born, weighing 9 lbs. The infant was the joy of Elizabeth's life, but disaster would strike again. Her child, the manifestation of the love she shared with her husband, took ill and died on September 20, 1864, before her first birthday.[183]

Elizabeth Carter Vincent

Elizabeth Carter Vincent was born in 1838 in Newark, New Jersey. Her mother died when she was just a child. Her father, Amos K. Carter, a successful businessman, in 1843 sent her to a girls' school founded by Miss Porter in Farmington, Connecticut. In 1854, she graduated and stayed on to teach there. Sadly, her father, returning from Liverpool, England, was on the steamship Pacific that was lost at sea. In Strong Vincent she found not only a fine man, but a man whose family loved her as well. And when she lost him and then their child, it was a wonder that she could go on and keep faith. But go on she did, though she never remarried. Instead, she clung to her husband's family. A moving account of her life afterward was left by Col. Vincent's brother, Rev. Boyd Vincent, an Episcopal priest, then a Bishop, in his "Our Family of Vincents," a short historical piece which he published for private circulation:

> As she had no home of her own, my father told her that his home should always be hers; and from that time on until her death, she absolutely identified herself, as a daughter, with her great per-

> sonal attractiveness and her rare intellectual gifts and culture she was not only a constant inspiration to younger members of the family and to a large social group of earnest young Erie people but also threw herself with enthusiasm into all the church work.... One of the finest things in her life was her devotion to and care of our defective and dependent brother Ward. For fifty years she taught and trained him.[184]

In addition, Elizabeth Vincent wrote religious books and maintained an active correspondence with many of her husband's military counterparts like Gen. Joshua L. Chamberlain and Vincent's old bugler, Oliver W. Norton. Norton had become a successful businessman after the War and did his best to perpetuate the memory of Col. Strong Vincent and the 83rd Pennsylvania regiment by writing and speaking about his War experiences. He also assisted Mrs. Vincent in obtaining an increase in her widow's pension from the government. So thankful was she for his help that she left the sum of $250.00 to Norton in her will, "to be expended for the best cigars he can buy."[185]

Elizabeth Carter Vincent died on Thursday, April 14, 1914, and was buried on Easter Sunday from St. Paul's Cathedral in Erie, with her daughter and husband in the family plot.[186]

Colonel Joshua L. Chamberlain

After the Battle of Gettysburg, Col. Joshua L. Chamberlain participated in many other battles. He was severely wounded on June 18, 1864, at Rives' Salient near Petersburg, Virginia, when he was shot in the groin while leading a charge. General Ulysses S. Grant promoted him on the spot to brigadier general for gallantry — an extremely rare incident during the War.[187] The wound was thought to be fatal but somehow he survived. Again, at the Battle of Quaker Road, Virginia, on March 29, 1865, Chamberlain was wounded. A bullet struck him in the chest but was deflected by a book of field orders in his pocket. Once again he rose to lead the fight. For his gallantry on the Quaker Road, Chamberlain received a brevet to the rank of major general. Time and time again, he demonstrated tenacious leadership and was always at the front with his men.

But Chamberlain's supreme moment may have actually come not from his skill in tactics, but from his manner of heart, when he was selected to receive the colors of the South at the surrender of arms at Appomattox on April 12, 1865. After Generals Grant and Lee had departed after the official surrender on April 9, Grant to Washington, and Lee to Richmond, the details of the surrender of arms was left to subordinate generals. Chamberlain was selected to perform this duty. He took it upon himself to modify the proceedings.[188]

As the vanquished heroes of the South approached Appomattox, the Union men stood waiting, their lines dressed. Chamberlain's own telling of the matter is worth recounting:

> On they come, with the old swinging route step and swaying battle-flags. In the van, the proud Confederate ensign — the great field of white with canton of star-strewn cross of blue on a field of red, the regimental battle-flags with the same escutcheon following on, crowded so thick, by thinning out of men, that the whole column seemed crowned with red. At the right of our line our little group mounted beneath our flags, the red Maltese cross on a field of white, erewhile so bravely borne through many a field more crimson than itself, its mystic meaning now ruling all.
>
> The momentous meaning of this occasion impressed me deeply. I resolved to mark it by some token of recognition, which could be no other than a salute of arms…
>
> Instructions had been given; and when the head of each division column comes opposite our group, our bugle sounds the signal and instantly our whole line from right to left, regiment by regiment in succession, gives the soldier's salutation, from the "order arms" to the old "carry" — the marching salute. Gordon at the head of the column, riding with heavy spirit and downcast face, looks up, and, taking the meaning, wheels superbly, making with himself and his horse one uplifted figure, with profound salutation as he drops the point of his sword to the boot toe; then facing to his own command, gives word for his successive brigades to pass us with the same position of the manual, — honor answering honor. On our part not a sound of trumpet more, nor roll of drum; not a cheer, nor word nor whisper of vainglorying, nor motion of man standing again at the order, but an awed still rather, and breath-holding, as if it were the passing of the dead!"[189]

And thus he welcomed them back into the Union in a manner out of the realm of mere humanity but of another source sublime — the transcending veil of Christian brotherhood. Even today at Appomattox, the place is marked and the story told to perpetuate the memory of soldiers coming home.

After the War, Joshua L. Chamberlain entered politics and served four one-year terms as a Republican governor of Maine. He later became president of Bowdoin College, implementing many new and innovative programs — even one preparing young men for military responsibilities. All the while, he maintained contact with the many officers and men of the 20th Maine Regiment, like Capt. Ellis Spear, Lt. Holman Melcher, who after the War became a successful businessman and mayor of Portland, Maine, and Sgt. Andrew Tozier, who worked for Chamberlain at his home in Brunswick, Maine, for a while. Past military leaders, politicians and men of letters often passed through the doors of his home on Main St. and partook of his and Fanny's gracious hospitality. The parade included Generals Grant, Sherman, Porter, Warren, Sheridan, and others. Senators, congressmen, and governors discussed the problems of the day. Longfellow stayed at Chamberlain's home when he came back for the fiftieth reunion of his class at Bowdoin in 1875, to deliver his famous poem, "Morituri Salutamus."[190]

The "General," as he was affectionately called in later years, was an active participant in regimental reunions and activities and often spoke and wrote on the War. Always ready to help a veteran or surviving spouse in need, to obtain pension assistance when eligible, his friendship was highly coveted.

On August 11, 1893, some 28 years after the War, Joshua L. Chamberlain was given the Medal of Honor from a grateful nation, "for daring heroism and great tenacity in holding his position on Little Round Top against repeated assaults and carrying the advance position on Great Round Top." It was an honor both richly deserved and highly prized. Today, the Chamberlain Medal of Honor rests in the Bowdoin College Library, Special Collections, given to the Library by a Chamberlain descendant.[191]

Frances (Fanny) Adams Chamberlain died on October 18, 1905, at age 79, being of ill health in her latter years. And on February 24, 1914, Joshua L. Chamberlain died quietly of complications resulting from the old wound he had received at Petersburg in June 1864. It is quite possible that he is the last man known to die of wounds received during the Civil War. He was 85.[192]

Colonel Patrick H. O'Rorke

As soon as it was practical, Col. O'Rorke's body was removed from the field and placed on the porch of the Weikert farm house behind Little Round Top, then later removed about a mile and a half further south of the battlefield to the Lewis A. Bushman farm. Quartermaster William H. Crennell of the 140th New York noted in his diary that both Col. O'Rorke and Gen. Stephen H. Weed were buried "in rear of the house on the west side of the first apple tree." Their grave sites were marked in case the families of these gallant men should come to claim their bodies.[193]

Colonel O'Rorke's wife came to Gettysburg to claim her husband's body which was removed to Rochester, New York, for burial with full military honors. His body would be moved twice more before finding its final resting place in the Cemetery of the Holy Sepulchre, north of Rochester.[194]

Clara Bishop O'Rorke

Clara Bishop O'Rorke was born in Rochester, New York, on March 29, 1837. One year minus one day younger than Patrick, she was 26 at the time of his death. As the War continued on, Clara cared for the sick and wounded soldiers in a soldiers' home in Rochester, doing more than her part in easing the pain and suffering of a war-torn nation. As the war neared its end, she entered the Novitiate of the Society of the Sacred Heart, Manhattanville, New York, on March 19, 1865, to become a Catholic nun. She took her first vows on March 21, 1867 in Kenwood, Albany, New York. Her final vows were taken on August 15, 1872, and she became Mother Clara O'Rorke. Two years later, she became Mother Superior of a convent in Detroit and then in Providence, Rhode Island, "where her influence was felt by everybody," teaching and administrating. She remained there until her death on February 18, 1893, a few weeks before her 56th birthday.[195]

Mother O'Rorke's obituary in the Providence Daily Journal, on February 21, 1893, described her as being "one of the best known members of her order in this country…greatly admired by her nobleness of character and her large-heartedness. She possessed a wonderful capacity for government and while enforcing discipline made everybody happy with whom she came in contact."[196]

General Gouveneur K. Warren

As the dust settled at Gettysburg, Gen. Meade saw an opportunity to recognize Gen. Warren's tactical genius and resolve as a battle commander. With General Hancock, the 2nd Corps commander, having been wounded on the third day of the fighting, while holding the line during Pickett's Charge, a new commander was needed. General Meade pressed for the selection of Warren for this post.

On August, 8, 1863, Warren recorded in his journal, "Today in Washington. Received appointment as Major General of Volunteers, to date from May 3, 1863. In the evening went to Baltimore."[197] No doubt he wanted to celebrate with his new bride, as a quick telegraph message to her was sent that day. "Emmie, I shall join you by the half-past six train." Not only was he being recognized for his outstanding performance at Gettysburg, but the Battle of Chancellorsville as well, noted by the back dating of his appointment to the date of the Chancellorsville clash. Within the space of 26 months he had risen from 2nd lieutenant to major general.[198]

General Warren's style of command was decidedly thoughtful, calculating, and methodical. It served him well throughout those coming months of the War with success after success, until Generals Grant and Sheridan took over command of the Army. They were different than Warren and soon developed the opinion that Warren was slow in placing his troops in motion, and into action. Their methods were more tenacious, so they thought, and also more costly in the loss of Union lives — but success covers many tracks.

Such was the case on April 1, 1865, at the Battle of Five Forks. Despite Union success, particularly of Warren's Corps, Gen. Sheridan, with approval from Gen. Grant, relieved Warren of command for being slow to support his cavalry units and further telling Warren that "he wasn't even in the fight!" Warren was dumbfounded and humiliated. His subordinate generals, Griffin, Chamberlain, and others were astonished as well, but they knew how jealously Sheridan guarded praise, wanting it mostly for himself. Sheridan could not bear the thought of giving the infantry credit for winning the battle or worse, rescuing his mounted cavalry. He possessed a giant ego, and his wrath found its home on the shoulders of Gen. Warren. Sheridan, too, was a great leader of men, but it was clear that their leadership styles clashed. And in such a clash only one general would be allowed to stand supreme.[199]

Though many subordinate officers immediately, and even Gen. Meade later, petitioned Gen. Grant on Warren's behalf, Warren was reassigned to duty at Petersburg, Va., clearly away from the closing scenes of battle and glory at Appomattox just over a week later. General Warren spent the rest of his life, literally, trying to undo the wrong done to him by Sheridan that day. He stayed in the Army after the War, in the Engineer Corps, all the while trying to get a military court to hear his case. It was a long time in coming, too, as Sheridan's popularity propelled him to higher command and not long after the War Gen. Grant became president. But after fourteen hard years of waiting, a court of inquiry was convened to consider the matter on December 11, 1879.[200]

The testimony given the court was long and telling, as Warren's good friend, Albert Stickney of New York, presented his case. And one by one the heroes of the Civil War told what they knew of the circumstances resulting in Warren's relief from command. Sheridan, ex-President Grant, Chamberlain and many others testified during the long, drawn out affair. A finding was not made known until November 21, 1882, when the War Department issued the order. While it would not censure Sheridan or Grant, it was what Warren needed. It was best summed up by Joshua L. Chamberlain:

> The traditions of the whole War Department were for sustaining military authority. We would not expect a Court to bring in a verdict of censure of General Sheridan or anything that would amount to that. We can only wonder at the courage of all who gave Warren any favorable endorsement or explanation. Let us remember that all the members of the Court were Regular officers with their careers to think of, that Sheridan was a Lieutenant General and soon to take command of the Army. But — what a triumph for true courage![201]

As for the charges levied against Warren, they were all denied. At last he was vindicated. But on August 8, 1882, three months before the findings were made public and he could stand triumphant, Gouverneur Kemble Warren died with a broken heart. "Ironically, those who kept vigil with him, waiting for the distant, silvery trumpet to sound taps, heard it and have remembered: 'The flag!' murmured Warren, just before he closed his eyes. 'The flag!'" He closed his eyes to life in Newport, Rhode Island, surrounded by a loving family. He was only 52.[202]

Sergeant Andrew Tozier

Immediately after the Battle of Little Round Top, Col. Chamberlain faced the problem of replacing officers lost during the battle. Remembering Tozier's bravery, Chamberlain recommended him for promotion to the rank of lieutenant. Tozier declined the promotion, saying that he did no more than a soldier's duty in guarding the colors during the battle. Chamberlain, honoring his humble request, rescinded the recommendation the next day.[203]

In May 1864, during a fight on the North Anna, Sgt. Tozier was wounded for a second time. This time he was shot above the left temple. Surgeons removed fragments of the bullet months later, but the lingering effects — ringing ears, dizziness, headaches — remained with him for decades. Andrew served out his enlistment and was mustered out of the service on July 15, 1864, as a sergeant. He had met his responsibilities.[204]

Sometime after the War, Andrew returned to his birthplace, the Litchfield-Monmouth area of Maine and there married Elizabeth (Lizzie) Bolden. In 1866, a son, Andrew Jr., was born to them. The 1870 Census records show that Andrew and Elizabeth were employed and lived as "domestic servants," in the Brunswick, Maine, home of his former colonel, who after the War became governor of Maine. While Chamberlain was governor he took up residence in Augusta, some 30 miles north of Brunswick, leaving his wife Fanny back home with the Chamberlain children. Who better to leave the care of his family and home to than the keeper of the Colors at Little Round Top?[205]

Andrew participated in some Grand Army of the Republic reunions and activities. At the Grand Reunion of the Soldiers and Sailors of Maine held in Portland, Maine, on August 9-10 in 1876, Andrew took charge of Chamberlain's yacht and conducted an hour-long sail for the boys. It appears that he maintained some friendships with the men, especially Gen. Chamberlain.[206]

By 1880 the Toziers moved to Cumberland, Maine, where Andrew took up farming and another child, Grace, was added to their family. Sadly, Grace died at the age of 8.[207] And in 1890, another move was made, this time back to the area of his birth in Litchfield. Andrew's son obtained a farm next door to his parents and started raising a family of his own.[208]

Many years after the War, Gen. Chamberlain's thoughts kept bringing him back to Little Round Top. He could always visualize Sgt. Andrew J. Tozier clearly — steadfast at the Colors, holding the center — not to be broken by the gray line advancing. He penned a recommendation to the Secretary of War asking that the highest token of respect — a Medal of Honor for conspicuous gallantry at Little Round Top Gettysburg — be given as reward for Sgt. Tozier's efforts on the field that day.[209]

So, a nation's salute was given, dated August 13, 1898, some thirty-five years after action — to a man most deserving. Andrew was 25 years old on that blustery day at Gettysburg. He was 60 when the medal arrived by registered mail, for which he signed the acknowledgment of receipt. There was no great band playing for him at that moment, but perhaps he could hear the guns at Gettysburg from afar and the bullets whizzing by as images of fallen comrades came to mind. Surely, he must have clutched that Medal close to his breast in their memory. He died quietly in Litchfield on March 28, 1910. A handsome headstone marks the spot where he rests.[210]

It is ironic that no "sure" photo of Andrew J. Tozier seems to have survived. But that matters little, for when we look for the "face" of heroism we may find it on anyone. Many mothers' sons or daughters have lifted up to that level of courage but have done so out of the view of recognition. In this regard, Andrew J. Tozier stands for much more than just that one moment on Little Round Top, where he stood firm and fought above and beyond the call of duty. Other members of the color guard, Pvt. Elisha Coan and Cpl. Charlie Reed did their part as well. And Cpl. Melville C. Day laid down his life for the colors and the cause there. So, absent a true picture of Andrew, the best we can do is to try to snatch the moment that Col. Chamberlain described of Tozier, with the colors clutched to his side with one hand and a gun blazing away with the other, straining to hold that center, and through the purple pall of battle the image emerges. And somehow, we may begin to feel that we may have seen someone like him somewhere before — in that War, or another War, or on the face of a Fireman, a Policeman or a soldier — man or woman — of today. Each one a hero!

LITTLE ROUND TOP TALK

Students and enthusiasts of that portion of the battlefield known as Little Round Top have debated some important and some not so important points of the action there. A few topics of particular interest will be explored in this section — which this writer hopes will encourage the reader to consider while walking upon that field, or as an armchair enthusiast, discussing with others the action of that day.

Where Did Vincent Fall?

Visitors to the Gettysburg Battlefield in search of the place where Vincent fell, will easily find a large boulder on the southern slope of Little Round Top, about one quarter of the way down the hill, in the area occupied by the 44th New York Infantry during the battle, upon which a small stone marker has been erected. Bearing the Maltese Cross insignia of the Fifth Corps, the marker states simply, "Gen. Strong Vincent, wounded July 2, Died July 7, 1863." It is regarded by Gettysburg officials as the first monument placed on the battlefield, other than those found in the National Cemetery. It was erected there, on the spot believed to be the place where Vincent fell, by representatives of Strong Vincent Post #87, of Erie, Pennsylvania, on July 25, 1878.[211]

Years later, an inscription was found on top of another large boulder just north of the 44th New York Monument on Little Round Top, indicating another place where Vincent fell. This was first reported as having being seen in October 1864 by Isaac Moorhead, a native of Erie, Pennsylvania, and was recorded in a sketch he later wrote of his life. To view it, one must climb atop the boulders as it is not visible from the ground. As a result, most visitors miss it. And this is too bad, for it is certainly worth a look. A careful climb will reward the enthusiast. The inscription on the stone reads:

Col. Strong Vincent fell here
Commanding 3rd Brig 1st Div 5th Corps
July 2d 1863

An investigation into the matter stated that the Vincent "rock" inscription was made by "representatives of the Memorial Association under the direction of members of the 83rd Pennsylvania." Its early date and approval by Memorial Association members weigh heavily in establishing its validity.[212]

Vincent's bugler, Oliver W. Norton, believed that the site on top of Little Round Top, where the large boulder is inscribed is likely the true spot, or near it, where Vincent actually fell. Norton further believed that the site located down the slope on the south side of the hill is more in keeping with the position of Vincent's headquarters while on the hill, the spot Norton believes Vincent was first taken to after being wounded. As Vincent was conscious, he could have, for at least a while, still directed his troops from that point before being taken off the field and to medical aid.

Speaking of the rock inscription Norton later wrote, "That big rock will probably stand there as long as any of the monuments do. No man living can point out the exact spot where Vincent stood when he was shot. In my opinion it was very near this big rock." Perhaps several veterans recalled seeing Vincent back at his headquarters site, wounded, and assumed it occurred there. It was noted in the records that many of the 83rd Pennsylvania's veterans were not in agreement with the placement of the Vincent marker on the south slope.[213]

A strong case can be made that the Vincent rock inscription site is the true spot, near where he actually fell, when one considers the fact that Vincent was rallying his right, the faltering 16th Michigan, when he was wounded. The Vincent rock position is in agreement with this action, whereas the stone marker's position on the south slope is clearly out of view and about 150 feet further south, away from the action of the 16th Michigan. If the extant historical data concerning Vincent's last moments is correct, he was near the summit of the hill — in view — and commanding his brigade in a moment of peril at the then most critical part of his line.

It has even been surmised that Col. Vincent was struck by a sniper's bullet fired from Devil's Den. While this may be romantic

Photo by Author

The Vincent inscripton rock. Probably, near this large boulder located just to the north of the 44th New York Monument, Col. Strong Vincent fell mortally wounded on July 2, 1863.

exaggeration, these tales from veterans, place Vincent in an exposed position. This is less likely to have been the case, if the south slope marker site is correct.

After careful consideration, the evidence shows that Vincent fell at or near the site of the Vincent rock inscription, atop one of the few large boulders just north of the present day 44th New York Monument. And the Vincent marker, located on the southern slope of Little Round Top, is approximately the position of his command headquarters during the battle. Both sites are worth visiting, to honor a hero of Vincent's stature.[214]

Lieutenant Colonel Norval E. Welch

Students of Little Round Top have cast a suspicious eye at the actions of Lt. Col. Norval E. Welch at Gettysburg. And it is no wonder that they do. Some think he balked, or flinched at Gettysburg, cowering behind the hilltop after the line of the 16th Michigan began to crumble under the pressure of Texas rifles. Surely, Pvt. Oliver Norton, Vincent's bugler, thought so. Some think Welch was confused, and others think he actually reacted to some perceived orders shouted from a general on the hilltop, (supposed to be Gen. Weed, or Gen. Sykes, though neither was believed to be on the field at that moment), for Welch to pull back the 16th Michigan to a more defensible position near the crest of the hill. Probably, Welch was wishing for the latter, but found himself caught in the mix of the former and allowed more than a tinge of fear to control his actions for a moment. That is when mistakes are often made on the battlefield or on any other field in life. The immediate after-battle tension even among his own men is evidence that something went wrong with Lt. Col. Welch that day.

But Welch fully redeemed himself on other battlefields on other days and gained or regained the respect of his men. Then, on September 30, 1864, he made the supreme sacrifice while leading his men, first over the wall, waving his sword, at the Battle of Peebles Farm, Virginia. "A commission to him who first mounts the parapet!" he said. And as he went over the wall a Rebel bullet crashed into his brain. He was given a hero's burial in his hometown of Ann Arbor, Michigan.[215]

Ironically, it was noted by one researcher that Welch's enlistment had expired just prior to his last battle, and he had chosen to remain with his regiment while awaiting his discharge. Perhaps this gives another glimpse into the true mettle of the man. In the face of battle, a true leader wants to be in the fray.[216]

After the War, Joshua L. Chamberlain considered the actions of men perhaps like Welch who had some bad moments in battle, but had many good ones as well, and ultimately died for the Cause. "...Among these men were some doubly deserving — comrades whom we thought lost, bravely returning... If sometimes a shadow passes over such spirits, it needs neither confession nor apology." His remark particular to Welch is worth review. "...Welch, of the 16th Michigan, first on the ramparts at Peebles' Farm, shouting 'On boys, and over!' and receiving from on high the same order for his own daring spirit..."[217]

The Oates Monument

For many years after the War, Col. William C. Oates tried in vain to have a monument erected at Little Round Top for his regiment. Certain guidelines had been set up by the Gettysburg Battlefield Commission. These allowed for monuments to the Union and Confederate regiments to be placed on the line of battle. Subsequently, a monument to the 15th Alabama regiment was located on what is now West Confederate Avenue, the "step-off" point of the regiment about three quarters of a mile away from where they wound up on Little Round Top. Neither did the Commission want to set a precedent by allowing Oates, then a Congressman, to set another marker at the Little Round Top site. The reason was obvious. It might have caused an explosion of other requests from other Confederate Memorial Associations, and the results would have been chaos; a battlefield so heavily marked and memorialized that no one could hope to make any sense of it. But they did cordially consider his request. Colonel Oates was even willing to pay for the monument himself.[218]

The sketch of the battlefield positions which Oates provided to the Gettysburg Battlefield Commission in 1905, in an effort to select an appropriate site for a monument to the 15th Alabama, describes with three "x's," places which Oates believed his men had reached in the attack. (See sketch.) It appears that Oates' men almost had the 20th Maine surrounded. Chamberlain was in disagreement with any such description, as not being true to fact. Oates' northernmost mark, probably where he believed Capt. De B. Waddell's men made their attack, clearly shows a threat of enveloping the Union line. Perhaps a few of Waddell's men did make it that far, but not enough of them to have been effective, for the 20th Maine line would have then collapsed. History tells us otherwise.[219]

Oates persisted in his request for years. All he wanted was to place a "little witness," a marble shaft, some fourteen inches at its base, six feet tall, to stand at a point he was sure his men had reached. After having submitted a map, marking a few points of his advance, any one of which was an acceptable site to him to place the marker, he reflected in a letter probably what his heart best felt: "There is a boulder upon the slope, thirty steps perhaps to the west or inside, the extreme line held by the 20th Maine. I remember distinctly an inci-

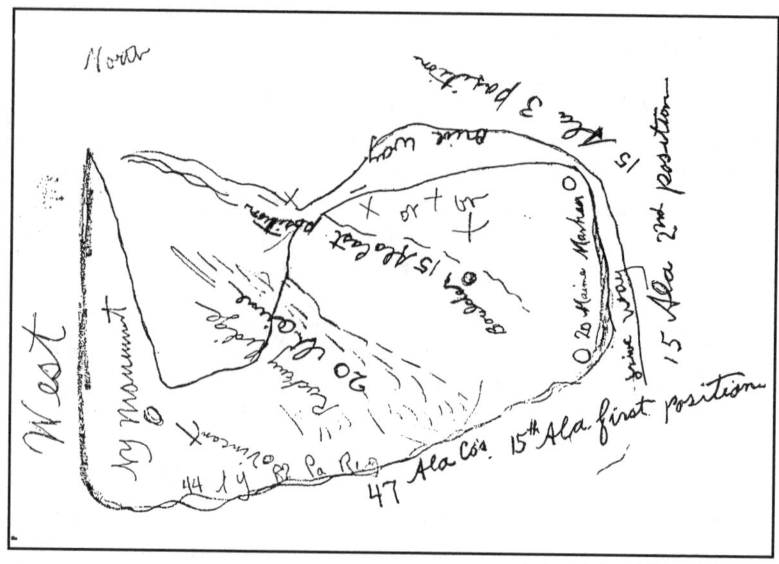

Gettysburg National Military Park Library

dent which occurred at that boulder where the colors of my regiment were at that time. Would your Commission agree for the shaft to be erected there?"[220]

Oates even sought the support and approval of Col. Joshua L. Chamberlain, his former adversary in the battle, in his effort to get permission to erect the monument on Little Round Top. Chamberlain had no problem with the placement of a monument honoring the 15th Alabama on Little Round Top, but he was careful to state that it should properly reflect the actual position attained by the 15th Alabama men. "I am more than willing that the monument of the 15th Alabama should be placed inside my lines, for some of these men were doubtless there, and I should feel honored by the companionship of the monument of so gallant a regiment on that historic crest, as I was honored by its presence forty years ago..." Chamberlain wrote in a letter to Col. John P. Nicholson of the Gettysburg Battlefield Commission. "The matter is in your charge, not mine. All I could wish is that they be placed in accordance with historic truth."[221]

Oates' intended inscription on the monument was:

To the Memory of Lt. John A. Oates
and his gallant Comrades
who fell here July 2nd, 1863.
The 15th Ala. Regt., over 400 strong,
reached this spot, but for
lack of support had to retire.
Lt. Col. Feagin lost a leg
Capts. Brainard and Ellison
Lts. Oates and Cody and
33 men were killed, 76 wounded
and 84 captured.
Erected 39th Anniversary of the battle
by
Gen. Wm. C. Oates
who was colonel of the Regiment

But the monument was never erected. Oates grew old and tired, and just ran out of time. He died in Montgomery, Alabama, on September 9, 1910. The former ruffian, turned lawyer and Confederate officer, who lost his left arm near Fussell's Mill, Virginia, on August 16, 1864, while leading his regiment, was no more. A man who after the Civil War became a Congressman, then Governor of Alabama, and served as a brigadier general during the Spanish American War, was denied his last wish — to see that "little witness" there on Little Round Top, a reminder to those visiting upon that field that the 15th Alabama made it — to "this" spot.

The large boulder to which Oates referred is still there today, on that bent back Union left! And resting upon it, the battlefield tramper of today will know that the colors of the 15th Alabama rested there. But once turned back by the mighty thrust of Union troops, in their legendary pivoting, "swinging gate" movement, all hope was lost. And with it went the hopes of the Confederacy on July 2, at Little Round Top at Gettysburg.

Col. William C. Oates' letter to Col. H. R. Stoughton

The letter on the following pages was written by Col. Oates when he was just shy of his 55th birthday. At this time in his life, he served in Washington as a Congressman for Alabama's Third District. As flamboyant a writer as he was a leader on the battlefield, a politician, and later governor of Alabama, Oates was full of color and energy. His classic book, *The War*, is still popular. This complimentary letter to Col. H. R. Stoughton of the 2nd U.S. Sharpshooters at Gettysburg is important. Some of the facts may be called into question, but the main point of the letter deals with the "effectiveness" of the 2nd U.S. Sharpshooters fire which resulted in diverting two Alabama regiments away from the "main thrust" of the Confederate attack, a fact which was critical to the Union victory! Here, the actions of Lt. Seymour F. Norton, and some 12 or 15 men from Company B, helped to turn the tide on Little Round Top.

—Abbeville, Ala., Nov. 22, 1888

Colonel H. R. Stoughton: — My regiment, 15th Alabama, was on the right of the Confederate line of battle. The position from which we advanced was at or near an old hedge row, north of the pike Emmitsburg, I believe, and right at the brow of the ridge south of Round Top. My orders were to guide to the foot of Round Top and hug to its base, keeping to the west of it and passing up the valley between it and Little Round Top, to find the Federal left and turn it if possible, and to go as far as I could. The lieutenant-colonel, Bulger, commanding the 47th Alabama regiment, was directed to keep close to me. This line of advance was a converging one, and had it not been disturbed by the presence of your command when it first appeared would have strengthened as we advanced, and our losses would not have produced any gaps or breaks in our line. The advance began, and when the right of my regiment approached the first foot of Round Top, we received your fire nearly in flank; our advance of 150 yards further without change of direction would have presented my right flank to your left, had your line been parallel; but as your right was retired in conformity to the ground, you had partly a front and partly a right oblique fire on me. Receiving no orders, I did not vary my course until you gave me a second one, which wounded several of my men, among them my lieutenant-colonel, Isaac B. Feagin, who lost a leg, and he now lives at Union Springs, Bullock county, Alabama. I then, knowing that it would not do to pass and leave you on my right and rear, gave the command, "Change direction to the right," and swung around far enough to advance on you, and the 47th Alabama swung with me. My advance dislodged you, but as you fell back up the south front of Round Top, you kept up a lively fire on my advancing line, which returned it but without much effectiveness, as your men, being trained sharpshooters and skirmishers, kept well under cover, taking advantage of the boulders which line the mountain side. When over half-way up your fire ceased, and henceforth to the top I did not see one of your men. *** I halted and rested for two or three minutes on the top of Round Top. My men were fainting with fatigue. We had marched 25 miles that day before going into the battle. I then advanced down the north side and to the east end of Vincent's Spur, where lay Vincent's brigade, the left of the Union line of battle, which I attacked and drove back upon the center, and my fire killed Gen. Vincent; but just as my ammunition was getting short, and when I was within 120 yards of Little Round Top, Lieut.-Col. Bulger (who now lives in Dadeville, Ala.; Mike Bulger is his name; he is now quite old and feeble) fell, severely wounded and his regiment, which had suffered severely, broke and retreated in confusion. A moment later you appeared directly in my rear and opened fire on me. I then occupied the ledge of rocks from which I had driven the 20th Maine. That and a New York regiment assailing me in front and you in the rear, forced my thinned ranks to face and fire in both directions, which we could not long endure. Half my men still able for duty were without ammunition. Two of my captains came and suggested a retreat. I ordered them to return to their respective companies and sell out as dearly as possible. But a little reflection made it appear as my duty to order a retreat, which I did, and we ran up the mountain and halted on the top for some time, and at deep dusk we moved back to an old house near the line of our advance, where we bivouacked for the night. Mine was the largest and best drilled and disciplined regiment in Hood's division. It went in with two field officers, 42 company and staff officers, and 644 men with arms in hand, and got out with one field officer, 19 company and staff, and 221 efficient men.

The great service which you and your command did was, first, in changing my direction, and in drawing my regiment and the 47th Alabama away from the point of attack. You drew off and delayed this force of over 1,000 men from falling on Vincent and the Union left at the same time of the attack of Law's other three regiments, the Texas and two Georgia brigades in front, and but for this service on your part I am confident we would have swept away the Union line and have captured Little Round Top, which would have won the battle for us. Again, when Vincent had fallen and I was within 150 yards of the top of Little Round Top, you forced me to retire by appearing in my rear and opening fire on me. The foregoing is substantially my recollection of you and your command at the great battle of Gettysburg. You and your command deserve a monument for turning the tide in favor of the Union cause. But after all, if Bulger had not fallen when he did, or if Longstreet had possessed less love for the fray and been at his proper place to have seen that we had Round Top, and had thrown a force on it and fortified it that night, the battle had been won for the Confederates. Meade testified that "with that which was the key-point in possession of the rebels, I could not have held any of the ground which I subsequently held to the last." Victor Hugo said: "Two great armies in battle are like two giants in a wrestle; a stump, a projecting root, or a tuft of grass may serve to brace the one or trip the other; on such slender threads does the fate of nations depend."

— Wm. C. Oates.

Source: Stevens, Capt. C. A., Berdan's United States Sharpshooters, Dayton, OH: Morningside. 1984 reprint., 326-329.

Oates, William C. *The War Between the Union and the Confederacy*. Dayton, OH: Morningside. Oates' date of birth, Nov. 30, 1833. Found in Introduction.

Dear Sir, "I had you perfectly certain."

During the battle of Gettysburg an unusual incident of more than curious proportions occurred. Years after the war, a Confederate soldier penned the letter below to Gen. Joshua L. Chamberlain, to tell him about it.

> Dear Sir,
>
> I want to tell you of a little passage in the battle of Round Top, Gettysburg, concerning you and me, which I am now glad of. Twice in that fight I had your life in my hands. I got a safe place between two big rocks, and drew bead fair and square on you. You were standing in the open behind the center of your line, full exposed. I knew your rank by your uniform and your actions, and I thought it a mighty good thing to put you out of the way. I rested my gun on the rock and took steady aim. I started to pull the trigger, but some queer notion stopped me. Then I got ashamed of my weakness and went through the same motions again. I had you, perfectly certain. But that same queer something shut right down on me. I couldn't pull the trigger, and gave it up,—that is, your life. I am glad of it now, and hope you are.
>
> Yours truly.

General Chamberlain included the story of receiving this letter from a Confederate veteran in his article, "Through Blood and Fire at Gettysburg," which was published in *Hearst Magazine* in May 1913. Regarding the letter, Chamberlain said in the article, "I thought he was that, and answered him accordingly, asking him to come up North and see whether I was worth what he missed. But my answer never found him nor could I afterwards."

Some historians have looked upon this report, and others like it, with suspicion. Whether this one is fact or fiction is for you to decide. As strange as it may sound, or curious as it may seem, it is true that such things have happened on battlefields before and since.

NOTE: There are several sources for this information. In the latest one, *Stand Firm Ye Boys From Maine* by Thomas Desjardin, p. 64, with endnotes on page 215 identify the writer of this letter as Herbert Heath of Alabama, in a letter dated February 7, 1903, in the MHS file.

Recommendation letter for Sgt. Andrew Tozier's Medal of Honor by Chamberlain.

Credit: National Archives. Andrew J. Tozier Medal of Honor file.

R.& P.515,221.

Case of

A N D R E W J. T O Z I E R,

late sergeant, Company I, 20th Maine Infantry Volunteers.

-ooOoo-

APPLICATION FOR A MEDAL OF HONOR.

Following is a copy of an application for the award of a medal of honor to this soldier, received at this office on the 31st ultimo:

"Brunswick, Maine, March 28, 1898.

"To the Honorable,
"The Secretary of War,
"Washington, D. C.
"Sir:-

"I have recently had occasion to examine with some care the private records of my late commands in the war for the Union. In reviewing the action of the Twentieth Regiment, Maine Volunteers, at Gettysburg, July 2, 1863, I came upon my minutes of the behavior of Color Sergeant Andrew J. Tozier, who stood at the angle of my line when I found it necessary to refuse my left wing in meeting the assault of Law's Brigade of Hood's Division, attempting to turn my position. In the sharp and long continued struggle our center was several times borne back, and the ground was finally carried by a bayonet charge.

"At a crisis of the engagement when our whole center was for a moment broken and the enemy seemed about to overpower us, I saw, as a thick cloud of smoke lifted, Sergeant Tozier standing alone at his advanced post,--the two center companies having lost nearly half their numbers, and the color guard entirely cut away,--the color staff rested on the ground and supported in the hollow of his shoulder, while with a musket and cartridge box he had picked up at his feet, he was defending his color; presenting a figure which seemed to have paralyzed the enemy in front of him, who might otherwise have captured the color.

"This was the object which I made the rallying point for the Regiment, and the center guide for the following charge.

"I made no more special mention of this in my official report, as I thought then that no one there had done more than a soldier's duty, and Sergeant Tozier in that feeling declined the promotion I offered him to a lieutenancy. I feel now, however, that his conduct was somewhat beyond what could have been required and expected as a part of duty; and I therefore desire to make this known as a part of his record at the Department of War; and I respectfully recommend that a medal of honor be awarded to Color Sergeant Andrew J. Tozier of the Twentieth Regiment, Maine Volunteers, for distinguished personal gallantry in defending the colors of that Regiment in the battle of Gettysburg, July 2d, 1863.

"I have the honor to be, with high respect, your obedient servant,

"Joshua L. Chamberlain,
"Lately Colonel, 20th Regt. Maine Vols.
"(Brvt.Major Genl., U. S. V.)"

The Mystical Chords of Memory

Excerpted from "Through Blood and Fire at Gettysburg," by Joshua L. Chamberlain, which first appeared in *Hearst's Magazine*, (June 1913), 50 years after the battle. Reprinted by *Gettysburg Magazine*, January 1, 1992. It is not only a fine piece of writing, but highly recommended reading — especially when visiting upon those scenes.

> ... I went — it is not long ago — to stand again on that crest whose one day's crown of fire has passed into the blazoned coronet of fame; to look again upon the rocks whereon were laid as on the altar the lives of Vincent and O'Rorke, of Weed and Hazlett — all the chief commanders. And farther on where my own young heroes mounted to fall no more [Charles W.] Billings, the valor of whose onward-looking eyes not death itself could quench; [Warren L.] Kendall, almost maiden-sweet and fair, yet heeding not the bolts that dashed his life-blood on the rocks; Estes and [Sgt. Charles W.] Steele, and Noyes and [Sgt. George W.] Buck, lifted high above self, pure in heart as they that shall see God, and far up the rugged sides of Great Round Top, swept in darkness and silence like its own, were the impetuous [Arad H.] Linscott halted at last before the morning star.
>
> I thought of those other noble men of every type, commanders all, who bore their wounds so bravely — many to meet their end on later fields and those on whose true hearts further high trusts were to be laid. Nor did I forget those others, whether their names are written on the scrolls of honor and fame, or their dust left on some far field and nameless here nameless never to me, nor nameless, I trust in God, where they are tonight.
>
> I sat there alone, on the storied crest, till the sun went down as it did before over the misty hills, and the darkness crept up the slopes, till from all earthly sight I was buried as with those before. But oh, what radiant companionship rose around, what steadfast ranks of power, what bearing of heroic souls. Oh, the glory that beamed through those nights and days. Nobody will ever know it here! — I am sorry most of all for that. The proud young valor that rose above the mortal, and then at last was mortal after all; the chivalry of hand and heart that in other days and other lands would have sent their names ringing down in song and story! ..."
>
> — Gen. Joshua L. Chamberbain

ENDNOTES

1. Glenn Tucker, *High Tide at Gettysburg* (Dayton, OH: Morningside Bookshop, 1983) 191-94.
2. Charles F. Johnson, *The Journal of Erie Studies* (Erie, PA: Erie County Historical Society, Spring 1988), 4.
3. *Ibid.*, 5-7.
4. *Ibid.*, 7.
5. Amos M. Judson, *The History of the Eighty-Third Regiment Pennsylvania Volunteers* (Dayton, OH: Morningside Bookshop, 1986), 81.
6. Elizabeth C. Vincent, "Letter to Miss Porter," copy in possession of Jim and Myra Wright.
7. Oliver W. Norton, *Attack and Defense of Little Round Top* (Dayton, OH: Morningside Bookshop, 1983), 285.
8. Judson, 115.
9. Emerson G. Taylor, *Gouveneur Kemble Warren: The Life and Letters of an American Soldier* (Cambridge, MA: Houghton Mifflin Co., 1932) 4.
10. *Ibid.*, 6.
11. *Ibid.*, 20.
12. *Ibid.*, 43.
13. *Ibid.*, 49.
14. *Ibid.*, 114.
15. *Bowdoin Magazine*, Vol. 64, No. 1 (Brunswick, ME: Spring/Summer 1991), 3.
16. Willard M. Wallace, *The Soul of the Lion* (Gaithersburg, MD: Ron R. Van Sickle Military Books, 1988), 16-19.
17. *Ibid.*, 28-31.
18. *Ibid.*, 34-38.
19. Joshua L. Chamberlain, "My Story of Fredericksburg," *Cosmopolitan Magazine* (Dec. 1912), 156.
20. John J. Pullen, *The Twentieth Maine–A Volunteer Regiment in the Civil War* (Dayton, OH: Morningside Bookshop, 1984), 23-27.
21. Alice R. Trulock, *In the Hands of Providence* (Chapel Hill, NC: University of North Carolina Press, 1992), 120.
22. Brian A. Bennett, *The Beau Ideal of a Soldier and a Gentleman* (Rochester, NY: Triphammer Publishing, 1996), 1-5; Norton, 288; McNamara, "Gettysburg Centenary Recalls Heroism of Rochester," *Catholic Council Journal* (Rochester, NY: June 28, 1963).
23. Donald M. Fisher, "Born in Ireland, Killed at Gettysburg: The Life, Death, and Legacy of Patrick Henry O'Rorke," *Civil War History*, Vol. XXXIX, No. 3 (OH: Kent State University Press, 1993), 227-28; Norton, 288; Bennett, 17-19.
24. Bennett, 22-24; *U. S. Military Academy Register*–Patrick H. O'Rorke and George A. Custer entries.
25. Bennett, 39-42.
26. McNamara; Bennett, 8, 62.
27. McNamara.
28. Bennett, *Sons of Monroe: The History of the 140th New York* (Dayton, OH: Morningside Press, 1992), 205; Bennett, "Beau Ideal" 114.
29. Andrew Tozier, Medal of Honor File, NARA; Sylvia Sherman letter re: Andrew Tozier, Maine State Archives.
30. Thomas A. Desjardin, *Stand Firm Ye Boys From Maine* (Gettysburg, PA: Thomas Publications, 1995), 24.

31. Pullen, 78-80.
32. Desjardin, 24.
33. Judson, 123.
34. *Ibid.*, 123-24.
35. Pullen, 95.
36. Wallace, 79; Joshua L. Chamberlain, "Through Blood and Fire at Gettysburg," *Hearst Magazine*, June 1913, 896.
37. Wallace, 79; Chamberlain, "Through Blood and Fire at Gettysburg,"896.
38. Bennett, *Sons of Monroe*, 203;
39. Edwin B. Coddington, *The Gettysburg Campaign: A Study in Command* (Dayton, OH: Morningside Press, 1994), 334.
40. George G. Meade, Meade Circular dated June 30, 1863, *Official Records of the War of the Rebellion*, Vol. 27, Part 3, 415; Bennett, Sons of Monroe, 204.
41. Bennett, *Sons of Monroe*, 204-205; Farley, "Reminiscences, No. 9" *Rochester in the Civil War,* 218, also published in Norton's Attack and Defense, 125.
42. Bennett, *Sons of Monroe*, 205.
43. Harry W. Pfanz, *Gettysburg, The Second Day*, (Chapel Hill, NC: University of North Carolina Press, 1987), 201; Roebling to Smith, Letter dated July 5, 1913, Rutgers University.
44. Emerson G. Taylor, *Gouveneur Kemble Warren: The Life and Letters of an American Soldier* (New York and Boston: Houghton Mifflin Company, 1932), 119-120.
45. Pfanz, 201.
46. *Ibid.*, 201-206; Coddington, 331; Norton, 309, 330.
47. Pfanz, 208.
48. Norton, 263-64.
49. Pfanz, 207.
50. *Ibid.*, 208.
51. Norton, 264.
52. Norton, 264.
53. *Ibid.*, 264.
54. Wallace, 91; Chamberlain, *Through Blood and Fire*, 898-99.
55. Wallace, 91-92; Chamberlain, *Through Blood and Fire*, 898-99.
56. Norton, 265; Norton, "Army Letters" 167.
57. Howard Prince, "A Probable Theory," *Lincoln County News*, May 22, 1883; Norton, 219, 242, 245; William B. Styple, *With a Flash of His Sword* (Kearny, NJ: Bell Grove Publishing Co., 1994) 59.
58. Judson, 125, 132; Chamberlain, *Through Blood and Fire*, reprinted in *Gettysburg Magazine* Jan. 1, 1992, 48; Norton, 265; Styple, 48.
59. Wallace, 92; Judson, 129.
60. Wright, "Time on Little Round Top," *Gettysburg Magazine*, Jan. 1, 1990, 53; Norton, 246.
61. Pfanz, 158, 162-64; J. B. Polley, *Hood's Texas Brigade*, reprint (Dayton, OH: Morningside Press, 1988), 159-62.
62. Pfanz, 158, 161-62.
63. *Ibid.*, 159; William C. Oates, *The War Between the Union and the Confederacy* (Dayton, OH: Morningside Book Shop, 1985), 211.
64. Oates; LaFantasie, "The Other Man," *Military History Quarterly*, 1993.
65. Oates, 674.
66. *Ibid.*, 212.
67. *Ibid.*, 297, 208.
68. Norton, report of Maj. J. M. Campbell, 148-49; Robert Krick, *Lee's Colonels* (Dayton, OH: Morningside Bookshop, 1992), 207; "General M. J. Bulger, An Alabama Hero," *New Orleans Picayune*, Sept. 18, 1898.
69. Krick, 207; Bio sketch of Col. James W. Jackson, Military File, NARA, copy in Alabama State Archives; Willis Brewer, *Alabama: Her History, Resources, War Record, and Public Men* (Alabama, 1872), 660.

70. "General M. J. Bulger," An Alabama Hero, *New Orleans Picayune*, Sept. 18, 1898.
71. Desjardin, 40-41; "General M. J. Bulger"; *Memorial Record of Alabama*, Vol. II, 1893, 998-99.
72. Pfanz, 168; Norton, 234-36.
73. Stevens, *Berdan's Sharpshooters* (Dayton, OH: Morningside Press, 1984), 2-7, 245.
74. Oates, 210; Pfanz, 169.
75. Oates, 210.
76. *Ibid.*, 210, 589-90.
77. *Ibid.*, 210-11.
78. *Ibid.*, 210-11, 686,87; Styple, 53.
79. Stevens, 326-28; Oates to Stoughton, Nov. 22, 1888; Norton, 235.
80. Ward, "Incidents," *Confederate Veteran*, Vol. 8 (1900), 347; Norton, 234-35.
81. Norton, 235.
82. *Ibid.*, 143, 235.
83. *Ibid.*, 163; Pfanz, 214; Patterson, Biosketch of Lt. Col. B. F. Carter, File, 1993.
84. Patterson.
85. *U. S. Census*, 1860.
86. Patterson.
87. Polley, 177; Pfanz, 215.
88. West, *A Texan in Search of a Fight* (Waco, TX: J. S. Hill & Co., 1901), 87, 95.
89. Oates, 212.
90. *Ibid.*, 212-14; Coddington, 392.
91. Jacklin, "The Famous Old Third Brigade," War papers read before the Michigan Commandery of the Military Order of the Loyal Legion of the United States, Vol. II, 1893, 47. See also J.M. Gibney, "The Shadow Passing," *Gettysburg Magazine*, Jan. 1992, 37; Styple, 48, 49.
92. Eugene A. Nash, *A History of the Forty-fourth Regiment New York Volunteer Infantry in the Civil War* (Dayton, OH: Morningside Bookshop, 1988), 154; Pfanz, 214-15.
93. Nash, 144-45, 154; Pfanz, 214-15.
94. Judson, 127; Desjardin, 50.
95. Ward, 347-48.
96. Gregory A. Coco, ed., *Recollections of a Texas Colonel at Gettysburg-by Colonel Robert M. Powell, 5th Texas Infantry* (Gettysburg, PA: Thomas Publications, 1990), 14-16.
97. Judson, 126.
98. Wallace, 93; Styple, 59.
99. Tilberg, "Chapters in the History of the Battle of Gettysburg," GNMP files, 235; Judson, 126; Desjardin, 56-58.
100. Krick, 337.
101. Wallace, 93; Chamberlain, *Through Blood and Fire*, 902.
102. Wallace, 94.
103. Judson, 129; Oates, 215.
104. Wallace, 97; Desjardin, 61.
105. Chamberlain, *Through Blood and Fire*, 905.
106. Nash, 295.
107. Norton, 166.
108. Pfanz, 236.
109. Norton, 164.
110. *Ibid.*, 165.
111. Pfanz, 225-26.
112. *Ibid.*, 222; Norton, 219, 259; Edward Hill, "Address of Colonel Edward Hill at the Dedication of the 16th Michigan Monument at Gettysburg," *Michigan at Gettysburg*, 108-9; Partridge to Bachelder, March 31, 1866.
113. Norton, 218-20; Norton, "Army Letters," 388; Hill, 108-9.
114. Norton, "Army Letters," 363-4, 374, 386; Judson, 127-28.

115. Nash, 145; Judson, 128; Charles F. Johnson, "The Short, Heroic Life of Strong Vincent," *The Journal of Erie Studies*, Vol. 17, No. 1, Spring 1988, 23; James H. Nevins and William B. Styple, *What Death More Glorious: A Biography of General Strong Vincent* (Kearny, NJ: Belle Grove Publishing Co., 1997), 77.
116. Norton, "Army Letters," 386.
117. Bennett, *Sons of Monroe*, 207, footnote 26.
118. Pfanz, 223.
119. *Ibid.*, 224.
120. Bennett, *Sons of Monroe*, 210; Pfanz, 228.
121. Bennett, *Sons of Monroe*, 211.
122. *Ibid.*, 217.
123. *Ibid.*, 211-13.
124. *Ibid.*, 215; Norton, 139.
125. Hazen, *National Tribune*, Sept. 13, 1894.
126. Bennett, *Sons of Monroe*, 215-18; Norton, 139.
127. Pfanz, 238.
128. Nash, 223.
129. Chamberlain, *Through Blood and Fire*, 903.
130. *Ibid.*, 904.
131. Theodore Gerrish, *Army Life: A Private's Reminiscences of the Civil War*, reprint (Gettysburg, PA: Stan Clark Military Books, 1995), 108; Styple, 78; Desjardin, 63.
132. Gerrish, *Army Life*, 108; Styple, 78; Desjardin, 182, 185, 191, 193, 223, endnote 36. Private Gerrish, while being listed as a participant at the Battle of Gettysburg, was not actually present for duty at Gettysburg. His popularized account of that battle was written from second-hand accounts as told to him by veterans.
133. Wallace 97-8; Judson, 129; Maine Commissioners, *Maine at Gettysburg*, reprint (Gettysburg, PA: Stan Clark Military Books, 1994), 261.
134. Oates, 218, 226.
135. Wallace, 99; Chamberlain, *Through Blood and Fire*, 904-5.
136. Wallace, 101.
137. Oates, 221.
138. Taylor, 129; Pfanz, 224; A. P. Martin, "Little Round Top," *Gettysburg Compiler*, Oct. 24, 1899, 1.
139. Pfanz, 225; Norton, 300, 311.
140. Pfanz, 240; Bennett, *Sons of Monroe*, 219; Martin, 1.
141. Styple, 68; Gerrish, 109-10.
142. Chamberlain, *Through Blood and Fire*, 905-06.
143. Styple, 123; Chamberlain, *Through Blood and Fire*, 906.
144. Pullen, 124.
145. Note: Historians have not satisfactorily resolved the actual whereabouts of the two companies of skirmishers of the 16th Michigan. Lt. Col. Welch's report indicates they did initially go out on the left and never came back to the line. But his report is considered to be biased. Norton says that they never actually went out. Capt. Spear of the 20th Maine acknowledges the fact that the 16th Michigan was initially on the left, but nothing about the skirmishers. Most telling might be the after-battle report of Capt. Walter G. Morrill, who gives credit to the twelve or fifteen 2nd U. S. Sharpshooters who fell in with his men and is silent on any members of the 16th Michigan being there with him during the fight. Morrill's willingness to give credit to others is evident. It is probable that if any members of the 16th Michigan were in his vicinity during the fight, Morrill would have reflected the same in his report. It is unlikely that Morrill could have confused the 2nd U. S. Sharpshooters with other troops of his brigade either, as the 2nd U. S. Sharpshooters had special "green" uniforms, easily distinguishable from the standard Union blue. Though it is possible that some of the skirmishers did get left behind in the retreat back to the line, a consequence of some confusion during the battle, their

number could only have been a few. And if any of them did get left behind to subsequently fall in with Morrill's fighting group, they never recorded it in any report or letter home that has emerged to date. See Styple, 48-9, 59, 139; Norton, 218-20, 243; Oates, 218-19.

146. Pullen, 124-25; Oates, 219, 221; Judson, 130; Styple, 139, 143.
147. Chamberlain, *Through Blood and Fire*, 907; Oates, 771.
148. Oates, 220.
149. *Ibid.*, 221-22, 717.
150. *Ibid.*, 217; Chamberlain, *Through Blood and Fire*, 908; Desjardin, 119.
151. Coco, 16.
152. Judson, 132; Krick, 308-09.
153. Wallace, 103-04; Chamberlain, 908.
154. Nash, 300; Pfanz, 237.
155. Pfanz, 237; J. W. Steven, *Reminiscences of the Civil War* (Hillsboro, TX: 1902), 114-15.
156. Pullen, 226, 256; Desjardin, 191.
157. Chamberlain to Bachelder, Jan. 25, 1884; Coddington, 767.
158. Pullen, 130; Styple, 78; Desjardin, 84; Pfanz, 402; Coddington, 440-41.
159. Styple, 44; Desjardin, 84.
160. Oates to Chamberlain, March 8, 1897. Chamberlain initially reported capturing a Capt. Christian, but was later corrected by Col. Oates in the letter listed above, many years after the war; Desjardin, 84, 218. Because of the added difficulty in properly aligning the gun sights of a weapon in darkness, shooters have a tendency to focus on (or favor) the front sight and thereby lower the rear sight of the gun, making the path (or trajectory) of the bullet fired higher than desired. Also, problems with depth and spatial perception are commonly experienced in night shooting that further add to the difficulty of hitting a proposed target. As a result, accuracy is severely diminished in night shooting.
161. *OR*, 27, Vol. I, 625-654; *Maine at Gettysburg*, 260.
162. *Maine at Gettysburg*, 260; Coddington, 441; *OR*, 27, Vol. I, 625-26.
163. *Maine at Gettysburg*, 260; Desjardin, 84-5; Styple, 78, 129.
164. *Maine at Gettysburg*, 259-60; Coddington, 441; Pfanz, 402-3, note 48; *OR*, 27, Vol. I, 625-26, 659. In Col. Fisher's Gettysburg battle report, it seems that he is claiming more credit than he should for his men and himself. But in the closing paragraph of his report, "My brigade captured and turned in to the proper officer over 1,000 stand of arms, brought off over 200 wounded rebels, and buried 80 of their dead..." Fisher shows more precisely the actual role, one of a "mop-up" action, that his brigade played at Little Round Top, arriving after the bulk of the fighting was over. Col. Rice and Col. Chamberlain's telling of events from the Union standpoint are far more accurate.
165. *Maine at Gettysburg*, 260.
166. Bennett, *Sons of Monroe*, 219; Norton, 139.
167. Bennett, *Sons of Monroe*, 219.
168. *Ibid.*, 223.
169. Judson, 130-31.
170. Wallace, 108.
171. *Ibid.*, 107.
172. Norton, *Strong Vincent and His Brigade* (Chicago, IL: private printing by author, 1919), 9.
173. Norton, 244; Norton, *Strong Vincent*, 10.
174. Benjamin F. Partridge to John Robertson, Aug. 10, 1868. Michigan State Archives, RG 59-14, Box 108, folder 7; J. M. Gibney, "A Shadow Passing," *Gettysburg Magazine*, Jan. 1992; Nash, note is foreword by Gerald W. Pergande.
175. Pfanz, 205.
176. Judson, 139.
177. *Ibid.*
178. *OR*, 27, Vol. I, 1041.
179. *Report of Joint Committee on the Conduct of the War*, Washington, 1865, 492.

180. Longacre, *General John Buford* (Conshohocken, PA: Combined Books, 1995), 245. Stanton was reluctant in the making of deathbed promotions in general.
181. Judson, 140; Charles F. Johnson, "Elizabeth Carter," a biographical sketch prepared for Miss Porter's School at Farmington, Connecticut, 1991, 7.
182. Judson, 140; Nevins, 82.
183. Boyd Vincent, *Our Family of Vincents* (Cincinnati, OH: Stewart Kidd Co., 1924). A note on Blanche Strong Vincent's date of death, courtesy of Jim and Myra Wright, Vincent researchers. Letter and note in possession of author.
184. Boyd Vincent, 103.
185. Norton, "Army Letters," 362-63; Johnson, 8.
186. Boyd Vincent, 103.
187. McFeely & McFeely, *Personal Memoirs of U. S. Grant, & Selected Letters, 1839-1865* (Library of America, 1990), 601; Trulock, 467. Trulock adds, "According to Bruce Catton, who examined the original handwritten manuscript of Grant's *Memoirs*, the accolade to JLC was the last item Grant added to his book. Grant died less than forty-eight hours later, on July 23, 1885; he depended on his editor to insert the paragraph in the correct place in the finished work. (Catton, *U. S. Grant*, 179). Grant did tell JLC at one time that his was Grant's first battlefield promotion, but he recalled in his *Memoirs* that over a month before JLC's promotion, he had similarly promoted Col. Emory Upton of the 121st New York (Grant *Memoirs*, 2: 224-25)."
188. Wallace, 185-90.
189. J. L. Chamberlain, *The Passing of the Armies* (Dayton, OH: Morningside Bookshop, 1989), 259-61.
190. Wallace, 33.
191. Trulock, 367.
192. *Ibid.*, 371. In a note on page 530 she quotes historian Bruce Catton's *Survivor*, under "Postscripts" in *American Heritage*, Vol. 30, No. 1, Dec. 1978, 111.
193. Bennett, *Sons of Monroe*, 221-22.
194. Norton, 290.
195. Johnson, 6.
196. *Ibid.*
197. Taylor, 137.
198. *Ibid.*
199. Chamberlain, *Passing of the Armies*, 142, 151.
200. Taylor, 238.
201. *Ibid.*, 247.
202. *Ibid.*, 248.
203. Andrew J. Tozier, Medal of Honor file, NARA. Contains letter of recommendation for Tozier from Col. Joshua L. Chamberlain, to the Secretary of War dated March 28, 1896.
204. Desjardin, 125.
205. *U. S. Census*, 1870.
206. Styple, 247.
207. *U. S. Census*, 1880.
208. *U. S. Census*, 1890.
209. See Appendix for copy of Gen. Chamberlain's recommendation.
210. Tozier Medal of Honor file, NARA.
211. GNMP, Strong Vincent Marker file, *Star and Sentinel*, August 1, 1878.
212. GNMP, Strong Vincent Marker file; Caughey, "The Occasional Writings of Isaac Moorehead, With a Sketch of his Life," 1882. Story reprinted in *The American Magazine and Historical Chronicle*, Vol. 1, No. 2, Autumn-Winter 1985-86 (copy in Vincent Marker file).
213. Norton, "Army Letters," 374; GNMP, Strong Vincent Marker file.
214. Norton, "Army Letters," 374, 386-7.
215. Gibney, 42; Robertson, 370.

216. Gibney, 42, citing *Weekly Michigan Argus Newspaper* article of Oct. 7, 1864.
217. Chamberlain, *Passing of the Armies*, 21, 352.
218. Robbins to Oates, Oct. 1902, GNMP, Oates correspondence file. Also noted is a copy of the *Rules Concerning Monuments at Gettysburg*.
219. GNMP, Oates correspondence file.
220. Oates to Nicholson, Dec. 29, 1904. Reference to "little witness;" Oates to Nicholson, Nov. 4, 1903, GNMP, Oates correspondence file.
221. Chamberlain to Nicholson, Mar. 15, 1905, GNMP, Oates correspondence file.

Suggested Reading

Adelman, Garry E. *Little Round Top: A Detailed Tour Guide.* Gettysburg, PA: Thomas Publications, 2000.

Bennett, Brian A. *Sons of Monroe: A Regimental History of Patrick O'Rorke's 140th New York Volunteer Infantry.* Dayton, OH: Morningside, 1992.

_____. *A Beau Ideal Of A Soldier And A Gentleman: The Life of Col. Patrick O'Rorke From Ireland To Gettysburg.* Rochester, NY: Triphammer Publishing, 1996.

Coco, Gregory A., ed. *Recollections of a Texas Colonel at Gettysburg — by Colonel Robert M. Powell, 5th Texas Infantry.* Gettysburg, PA: Thomas Publications, 1990

Coddington, Edwin B. *The Gettysburg Campaign: A Study in Command.* New York: Charles Scribner's Sons, 1968.

Desjardin, Thomas A. *Stand Firm Ye Boys From Maine. The 20th Maine and the Gettysburg Campaign.* Gettysburg: Thomas Publications, 1995.

Judson, Amos M. *History of the Eighty Third Regiment Pennsylvania Volunteers.* Reprint. Dayton, OH: Morningside, 1986.

Nash, Eugene A. *A History Of The Forty-fourth Regiment New York Volunteer Infantry In The Civil War.* Reprint. Dayton, OH: Morningside, 1988.

Nevins, James H. and William B. Styple. *What Death More Glorious: A Biography of General Strong Vincent.* Kearny, NJ: Belle Grove Publishing Co., 1997.

Norton, Oliver W. *Attack and Defense of Little Round Top.* Reprint. Dayton, OH: Morningside, 1983.

____. *Army Letters 1861-1865.* Reprint. Dayton, OH: Morningside, 1990.

Oates, William C. *The War Between The Union And The Confederacy.* Reprint. Dayton, OH: Morningside, 1985.

Pfanz, Harry W. *Gettysburg, The Second Day.* Chapel Hill, NC: University of North Carolina Press, 1987.

Polley, J. B. *Hood's Texas Brigade.* Reprint. Dayton, OH: Morningside, 1988.

Pullen, John J. *The Twentieth Maine: A Volunteer Regiment in the Civil War*. Reprint. Dayton, OH: Morningside, 1984.

____. *Joshua Chamberlain: A Hero's Life & Legacy*. Mechanicsburg, PA: Stackpole, 1999.

Smith, Diane M. *Fanny & Joshua: The Enigmatic Lives of Fanny and Joshua Chamberlain.* Gettysburg, PA: Thomas Publications, 1998.

Styple, William B. *With A Flash Of His Sword.* Kearny, NJ: Bell Grove Publishing Co., 1994.

Taylor, Emerson G. *Gouverneur Kemble Warren: The Life and Letters of An American Soldier.* New York and Boston: Houghton Mifflin Co., 1932.

Trulock, Alice R. *In The Hands of Providence: Joshua L. Chamberlain & The American Civil War.* Chapel Hill, NC: University of North Carolina Press, 1992.

Tucker, Glenn. *High Tide At Gettysburg*. Bobbs-Merrill Co., 1958. Revised edition. Dayton, OH: Morningside, 1973.

Wallace, Willard M. *The Soul of The Lion: A Biography of General Joshua L. Chamberlain.* New York: Thomas Nelson & Sons, 1960.

INDEX

J

K

L

M

N

O

P

R

S

T

V

W

About the Author

After high school and serving in the U.S. Army in Vietnam, Ken Discorfano returned to his hometown of Lodi, New Jersey, and shortly thereafter joined the local police department, where he attended the Bergen County Police Academy to train as a police officer. He worked his way through the ranks to become patrol captain, commanding the patrol division of that department. Throughout his career he attended advanced training by state and federal agencies and became interested in team tactic operations for the department's local Emergency Response Team which he commanded for some years. This led to an interest in improving his leadership skills. During this invaluable study, Ken grew aware of the actions of Colonel Joshua L. Chamberlain of Gettysburg fame. A trip to Gettysburg made Ken an avid student of Chamberlain and the Battle of Gettysburg with a focus on Little Round Top. As a training officer for his department, he included some of the Chamberlain saga in classes, to inspire young officers to think, to be ready to take charge, and develop their own leadership skills.

Now retired, living in sunny Tucson, Arizona, enjoying other pursuits; writing, history, music, and astronomy — always trying to broaden his perspectives — seeing the world about him in a vivid light, Ken is still looking for new challenges. It is apparent that some of the old professor-turned-soldier from Bowdoin College, (Joshua L. Chamberlain), has rubbed off on him. And, for that, Ken says, "Thanks Lawrence!"

THOMAS PUBLICATIONS publishes books about the American Colonial era, the Revolutionary War, the Civil War, and other important topics. For a complete list of titles, please visit our website:

www.thomaspublications.com

Or write to:

THOMAS PUBLICATIONS
P.O. Box 3031
Gettysburg, PA 17325